Country Music's Hidden Gem

Published by WordCrafts Press
Cody, Wyoming 82414
www.wordcrafts.net

Country Music's Hidden Gem

The Redd Stewart Story

Billy Rae Stewart

with Gail Kittleson

WordCrafts Press

Dedication

This book is dedicated to my wife Sharon. Without her many hours of research, organization, and support, this book would not have been possible. She has been my rock throughout this process and my foundation for almost 50 years. I love you, babe!

I would also like to thank Gail Kittleson for sharing her expertise in this project. She has been our guiding light while writing this book. Thank you for being there for us.

Last but not least, I want to thank my family for living the life they did to give me this great story to write, and the fans who made it all possible.

~Billy Rae Stewart

Would it be that everyone could cross the path of one gentle and inspiring spirit? I am writing this, privileged to have stood in the light of such a man, an unassuming gracious soul that touched the lives of all who knew him personally, a great individual talent that would bless the world with his love for songwriting, music recordings and performances.

The journey begins as more than just a rags-to-riches story, but with an essential heritage of family love and music that would later shape the man into one of the world's greatest 'unsung heroes' of music influence. A life that inspired others to do better, be better, to love unconditionally and to share with others the blessing of God-given talent. A man who never asked for personal praise, but whose individual contribution to the Country and Pop music industry is still alive throughout the world today.

Many of his written songs have been performed and recorded by such entertainment legends as Patti Page, Hank Williams, Roy Rogers, Dean Martin, Michael Bublé, and the list goes on. He once said to me personally in all humility, "I don't deserve any of this."

Follow these pages of heartfelt thoughts about our subject as explored in detail by the musician, author and loving son of this sincere man, revealed for the first time is the real-life love story that inspired the lyrics to the world's most famous Country music song. Redd Stewart's accomplished career and talent shows he lived for the edification of his fellow man, by sharing his great talent and love for music.

Learn more about Redd Stewart at www.reddstewart.com.

~Kent Stewart

The Early Years

Henry with his first band - The Kentucky Wildcats

Henry with Cousin Emmy and Her Kin Folk

In 1923, America was booming. From 1920 to 1929, the economy grew by forty-two percent, so the era was referred to as the Roaring Twenties. World War I had ended and our soldiers returned home with new perspective, energy, and skills. America enjoyed its first taste of being a global power, and our economy grew like crazy.

This time birthed the automobile and airline industries, and mass production brought new consumer goods to American citizens. Washing machines, refrigerators, radios, and many more inventions became everyday household items. Expanding easy credit made all this possible, but along with banking and stock market policies, created a hidden storm that would bring about what we now refer to as the Great Depression.

This is where our story begins. So find a comfortable chair and grab a cup of coffee to embrace the tale of the man I call *Country Music's Hidden Gem*. I also had the privilege of calling this man my dad.

On May 27, 1923 just outside Ashland City, Tennessee, Samuel Lawrence Stewart and Lucy Jane Stewart gave birth to a baby boy, the third son in their growing family. They named him Henry Ellis Stewart.

Samuel made a living as a tenant farmer, and though the economy was booming, farming income fell by 21% while taxes per acre rose by 40%, which forced Samuel to supplement his income as a cook, cobbler and barber in nearby Nashville. But an event was coming that would not only change the lives of the Stewart family, it would set young Henry on a track towards a destiny awaiting him in Kentucky.

In 1929 the stock market crashed, starting a chain reaction that launched America into the Great Depression. With the economy collapsing around him, Samuel could no longer make ends meet. The situation forced him to move to Louisville, Kentucky to find a better job to support his family, which had now grown to four sons and one daughter.

Besides being a farmer, cobbler, cook, and barber, Samuel was also an excellent musical instrument maker, and Lucy just happened to be a musician who taught Samuel and the kids how to play. By this time, Henry's two older brothers were already playing music and would sing and play on street corners while they sold newspapers.

They were also featured on the local WHAS radio in Louisville after an article entitled, "Al and Slim, the Courier Journal Singing Newsboys," appeared in the newspaper. With the influence of his parents and brothers, it was only natural that young Henry would soon be performing as well.

It didn't take him long to figure out how to make money with his music. At a very young age, he would sit on the front porch of his childhood home and play the banjo his father had made. Lots of people would stop to listen and throw pennies into his straw hat. When he made enough money, he would run down to the local store to buy candy, then come back and play for some more.

Henry learned to play the banjo, guitar and fiddle like a pro and before long was giving his brothers a run for their money. Eventually the family boasted five boys and two girls, and each one played an instrument. They became the regular entertainment for family and friends at family gatherings. But young Henry was about to find a much bigger stage.

Meanwhile, welcome news came from south of the border in Tennessee. On November 28, 1925, George D. Hay founded the Grand Ole Opry as a one-hour radio barn dance on WSM. By 1930 the program reached thirty states with 50,000 watts of power.

The musicians had become a Saturday night tradition, playing what was known back then as Hillbilly music. Country music was

4

in its very early stages, and another young man in Abrams, Wisconsin named Julius Frank Anthony Kuczynski was navigating a collision course with Henry Stewart.

By 1929, young Frank was already testing his musical skills with his first band, Frankie King and the King's Jesters. He changed his last name to King at the advice of a friend and made the name legal when he married.

Frank's father played in a polka band and taught young Frank to play the accordion and fiddle after he taught himself to play the harmonica. Still in high school, Frank would milk cows in the morning, work for his uncle after school, and play music at night.

Little did Henry and Frank know that this new phenomenon branded Country music was about to change their lives forever! Destiny was bringing them together, and the combined musical skills they were learning would soon form a partnership that would last almost sixty years and make music history. These two would become known in certain music circles as "The Men with the Golden Pen."

Starting at such a young age and being surrounded by family members who were all talented musicians was a big advantage for young Henry and helped to hone his musical skills. Frequently, guests would come to visit and listen to all of the kids perform. In an interview with my Uncle Billy years ago, he said that the kids hated playing for people because they were all shy.

When guests would come over they would all hide in their rooms, but my grandfather would move all the furniture to the sides of the living room and yell, "It's not time for bed yet so you kids get your instruments and come play for everybody." There was a lot of dancing and shouting as the kids played their instruments.

The Stewart house was a busy place because my grandfather was always bringing people home who needed a place to stay and a good home-cooked meal. That's just the kind of guy he was. It was nothing to wake up and find strangers sleeping on the living room floor, and of course he would always have the kids play for them as well.

This provided great training for his children and helped them get used to playing in front of people, a skill they would all need for the future. All seven kids ended up playing professionally at some time. Three of them played on the Grand Ole Opry. Al and Slim, Redd's older brothers, the Courier Journal Singing Newsboys, played on local Louisville radio, and Al also played with a group called the Blue Velvets.

Gene played guitar on the Grand Ole Opry with Curly Fox and Texas Ruby. He also played standup bass and sang with Pee Wee King's Golden West Cowboys. Billy, Redd's younger brother, played fiddle on the Grand Ole Opry with Lonzo and Oscar at sixteen and was known as the youngest old-time fiddler on the Grand Ole Opry.

He also worked with Little Jimmy Dickens, Leon Short, and Smiley and Kitty Wilson. Redd's youngest sister, Mary played standup bass and sang with her sister Juanita on guitar and vocals. They were known as The Golden Girls.

Though each of his brothers and sisters were extremely talented, Henry excelled beyond the rest and became a part of Country music history. Being a lifelong musician myself and following the industry, I have learned that it takes more than just musical talent to rise above the others and be successful in the music business. You need to be a total package, as I like to call it. You need musical talent, performing talent, songwriting skills, the right personality, and a true desire to entertain people. My father made a total package, including a voice second to none.

Besides being a musical instrument maker, his father Samuel played the fiddle, banjo, and guitar. His mother played the banjo and guitar. It's no wonder my dad became a musician.

My father claimed his oldest brother, Al had the greatest influence on him. He told me that Al would get him started on a song using a metronome and then take it out of the room. Toward the end of the song he would bring it back in and if my dad was not still on time with the metronome, he would get mad as the dickens.

Al was a perfectionist and trained my dad to be the same. All these experiences as a young boy with his family prepared him for what was to come.

Over time young Henry kept developing his skills, and when he turned fourteen, he quit school and formed his first band with fellow members Rookie Kirk, Gilbert Stewart (no relation), and Billy Long. They called themselves the Kentucky Wildcats.

They used to do advertisements for the Ford Motor Company and did a show at their showroom on Fifth Street in Louisville, Kentucky. They also played on WGRC Radio in Louisville. It was during this time that Henry took on the nickname of Tiny due to his small size, and wrote his first jingle, a commercial for the Ford Motor Company. The jingle went like this:

> *Watch the Fords go by*
> *See them how they fly*
> *Full of pep and speed*
> *Always in the lead*
> *There must be a reason why.*

By 1939, Tiny Stewart was playing the fiddle for Cynthia May Carver, better known as Cousin Emmy. She was from Kentucky and one of Country music's pioneer women performers. The band called Cousin Emmy and Her Kinfolks ended up in Atlanta as the main act on The Crossroads Follies, a popular radio show on WSB and WAGA.

My dad said he learned a lot about performing from Emmy. She was a great entertainer and full of confidence on stage. But destiny was right around the corner for Tiny Stewart. Because of a chance meeting around 1937, something was about to happen that would change everything.

Meanwhile back in Abrams, Wisconsin, Frank was building a career of his own. Whether you call it luck or fate, Frank was about to take a phone call that would change the course of his life forever. While touring in Wisconsin, Gene Autry and his manager J.L. Frank were traveling through a city called Racine when one of their two Buicks was involved in an accident.

Four members of the band were injured and could not continue to the next show, and their car's fender was rubbing against a flat tire. They towed it to a local garage for repair, and while they waited, they heard Frank King & The King's Jesters playing on the Polish American Radio Show.

They liked what they heard, and in need of some musicians, called the station to hire the players to fill in on their next show. Frank and the band had finished the show and were on their way out the door when the phone rang. Frank reached down and picked it up. J.L. Frank asked to speak with the leader of the band, and Frank said, "That's me!"

Little did Frank know he was talking to his future father-in-law. Long story short, J.L. hired Frank and some of the band members to fill in on the next show. Once the show was over, he asked Frank if he would continue with performing for the remaining dates, and since the season was slow for the Jesters, Frank agreed. After the tour, Frank went back to the Jesters to play the ballrooms around the lakes for the summer, and J.L. Frank and Gene Autry returned to Chicago. But that was not the end of the relationship.

After summer was over, J.L. Frank asked Frank to join Gene Autry's band, the Range Riders. After playing with Gene's band for about two months on WLS radio, J.L. Frank and Gene decided they should move the band to Louisville, Kentucky to play on 50,000 watt WHAS Radio while Gene waited for a movie deal to come along.

During this time, Frank got the name Pee Wee. With three Franks in the band, J.L. Frank declared, "Since you're the shortest, we're going to call you Pee Wee." The name stuck. They played together for seven to eight months until Gene left for Hollywood around 1935.

Pee Wee then joined the Log Cabin Boys under the leadership

of Frankie More and played on WHAS for a year or so. There, he met his destiny in a chance encounter that would put him on the path to a long and prosperous career and form a friendship that would last a lifetime.

Redd joins The Golden West Cowboys

The Camel Caravan

Some people would say that a particular day in 1937 was just my father's lucky day, but I completely disagree. I believe Pee Wee King and my dad were brought together by God through the series of events you just learned. From the moment they met, they were like two peas in a pod.

Each one had a set of talents and skills, and one without the other simply didn't work, as you will see through the rest of the story. Though they were both highly talented, Pee Wee had some skills my father didn't, and Dad had some that Pee Wee lacked. They were a team made in heaven that worked like a well-oiled machine.

Now it's time to tell you how these two incredibly talented men got together. On a normal day in 1937, my dad was on his way to the WGRC radio station to play with his band. J.L Frank, Pee Wee's manager, stepped out the back door and saw my dad walking down the alley with his fiddle in a gunnysack.

Mr. Frank asked him, "What's your name and what do you do?"

My dad replied, "My name is Henry Stewart, and I play in a little country band called The Kentucky Wildcats."

Mr. Frank said, "How would you like to work with Pee Wee King?"

Dad replied very casually, "I wouldn't mind it."

Mr. Frank replied, "Well, when you finish your present job and want to go into business with Mr. King, we'll work it out."

Pee Wee's fiddle player was out due to a sickness in the family, so my dad filled in for him, and filled in a few more times after that when they needed some help, but though Mr. Frank wanted him to join the band full-time, Dad was not ready to give up his own band just yet. An interesting footnote here: at this particular time, Redd Stewart was giving serious consideration to becoming a minister.

Pee Wee and the band, now called the Golden West Cowboys, got a chance to audition for the Grand Ole Opry in Nashville. The audition started around 11:00 am. When it was finished, the band was asked to stay over and play the Grand Ole Opry that night, so they did.

The following day they returned to Louisville, knowing that in two weeks they would return as permanent members of the Grand Ole Opry. Pee Wee felt that their very polished performance was the reason the judges were so impressed. He and his band already knew studio work because of their time on the radio, which required them to be extremely organized in their performances. This wasn't their first rodeo!

The band made its debut appearance as new members of the Grand Ole Opry on the first Saturday of June 1937. The Grand Ole Opry at this time was at the Dixie Tabernacle on Fatherland Street in east Nashville. Although the audition went well, George D. Hay, whom they called the Solemn Old Judge, was not so impressed.

Up until now, most of the performers on the Grand Ole Opry were farmers who doubled as musicians on the weekends, so the show had a very simple, rural feel to it. Most of the performers wore bib overalls, and the music was called Hillbilly music.

Pee Wee and his band came from a completely different environment, playing at many vaudevilles and theaters. The band wore costumes that Pee Wee called 'western cowboy stuff.' Their matching outfits were very clean and flashy. At the time, the only other member of the Opry that dressed this way was Zeke Clements.

The boys in the band liked their costumes so much that they wanted to wear them out after the shows, but Pee Wee made them leave their clothes in the dressing room. Their performances were extremely polished and professional, which clashed with the Hillbilly performances of the local performers. Like I said, the Solemn Old Judge was not impressed and did not like the change.

The Grand Ole Opry paid $16 per show, and members were required to be there every Saturday night. This made it tough for their other performance schedule. But Pee Wee saw this as an opportunity to get into the movies because the Opry would give them permission to be absent if they were making a movie.

They would travel to Hollywood for about five weeks. Making a movie usually took two weeks, so the rest of the time they would play dates around the area to make more money. Their first screen performance was in Gold Mine in the Sky, a 1938 Gene Autry movie.

In 1940 Pee Wee and his band left the Grand Ole Opry and moved back to Louisville. J.L. Frank got the boys a morning show on Louisville's WHAS radio. When they weren't doing the radio show, Mr. Frank had them playing dances around the area. At one of those dances, a disc jockey introduced a young man named Eddy as "the latest thing in St. Louis."

This young man sang a couple of songs to such tremendous response that J.L. Frank hired him on the spot to be the lead vocalist in the Golden West Cowboys. Up to that point, Texas Daisy had sung the lead, but now Eddy Arnold took her place.

J.L. Frank decided it was time to expand the show by adding another old-time country fiddle player. The first name that came to his mind was my dad, Henry Stewart, whom he had met in the alleyway in 1937. By this time Henry had changed his name from Tiny to Redd because of his red hair and fair complexion. He made this name legal a few years later.

J.L. Frank went out to Redd's home and made his proposal for Redd to join the band. Still underage at this time, Redd needed his parent's consent. This is when Redd Stewart became an official member of the Golden West Cowboys, but America was about to be drawn into World War II, and Redd had no idea he was about to be drafted into the U.S. Army.

Prior to this, Pee Wee moved the band back to Nashville to rejoin the Grand Ole Opry. Around August 1941, WSM put together a show to send out entertainers from the Opry to entertain troops on military bases all over the United States and in Latin America. They called this tour the Camel Caravan, sponsored by Camel cigarettes. Around this same time, J.L. Frank called Minnie Pearl and asked her to go on the road with the Golden West Cowboys. He offered to pay her $50.00 per week.

The Camel Caravan actually started as a radio show and someone came up with the idea to go on the road to entertain servicemen at military bases around the country. The show was divided into three units, one based in Hollywood, one in New York, and the third in Nashville. Mr. Frank persuaded the advertising firm that ran the show to add Pee Wee's show to the Nashville unit.

Included in the show were several pretty young girls wearing very skimpy outfits. They would walk through the crowd before each show, passing out samples of Camel cigarettes to the servicemen. Minnie Pearl got paid an extra $50.00 a week to chaperone these four cigarette girls.

Camel Caravan was credited with covering more than 50,000 miles in nineteen states and performing 175 shows in 68 Army camps, airfields, and naval and marine bases. Unfortunately, Redd was only involved in the first couple of shows. Shortly after starting with the Camel Caravan, he was drafted and sent to the South Pacific.

Redd in his uniform

Redd in his uniform

SOLDIER'S LAST LETTER

Words and Music
by
ERNEST TUBB
and
Sgt. HENRY STEWART

When drafted in 1941 after the attack on Pearl Harbor, my father weighed only 116 pounds at 5'3"—hardly a candidate for a soldier. He started his military training at Camp Forrest in Tennessee, where he traded in his fiddle for a rifle and a pair of combat boots. Camp Forrest was located in Tullahoma, and became one of the U.S. Army's largest training bases during World War II.

In 1940 the United States began limited preparations for war and established Camp Forrest as a draftee training facility. The projected $13 million facility was expected to cover forty thousand acres, but eventually Camp Forrest cost $36 million and covered 78,000 thousand acres. Housing at the induction and training center proved to be a recurring problem, and many soldiers bivouacked in tents.

Camp Forrest employed 12,000 civilians who ran the post exchanges, operated the 9,000 square-foot laundry, performed maintenance on military vehicles, repaired tanks and artillery pieces, and staffed the induction center where some 250,000 young men received their initial U.S. Army physical exams.

Between 1941 and 1946, Camp Forrest was an active army post, and officially became a prisoner of war camp on May 12, 1942. The camp housed Italian and German POWs who became laborers in camp hospitals and on farms in the local community.

My dad was sent to New Guinea, an island just north of Australia. The stage he would be performing on now would be quite different than the Grand Ole Opry and would require a different set of skills for the New Guinea campaign from 1942–1945.

When the Japanese finally surrendered, this campaign had resulted in a crushing defeat and heavy losses for the Empire of Japan. As in most Pacific War actions, disease and starvation claimed more Japanese lives than enemy fire.

I was told Dad served as a tank radioman during his time in the service, but this was something he never talked about. Most of what we know comes from family members. Dad's group followed Recon when entering a territory, so he likely saw plenty of action. He hated violence and every minute of the war.

While stationed there with the rank of sergeant, influenced by the devastating scenes of jungle warfare, Dad wrote the song, "Soldier's Last Letter," which Ernest Tubb worked on and recorded in 1944. It became a No.1 hit, remaining at the top for four weeks out of a seven-month stay on the Country charts and crossing over to the Pop chart Top 20.

In 1962 during the Vietnam War, the Louvin Brothers covered the song and included it in their album *Weapon of Prayer*. Again, the recording rose to the top of the charts, as the song truly pictures the pain war had caused to millions of people. Merle Haggard's version, part of his album *Hag*, peaked at No. 3 in the U.S. Billboard Hot Country Songs in 1971.

My dad had no idea that his beautiful tribute song would sadly continue as an anthem for many fallen heroes to come. Over the years we have received many stories from people who have been affected by "Soldier's Last Letter." The following is one:

"I love Redd's voice and have always loved "Soldier's Last Letter." I was in the military, and even though I never saw combat, I did see friends not make it home, so that song kind of reminded me why we traveled so far at the risk of never coming back. God bless y'all for keeping your father alive with his music. Can't wait to meet him when we're called to glory. It'll be one big sing-along!"

~Robert Clarkson, Eagleville, Tennessee

One of Redd's custom-made outfits

On August 6, 1945, the United States shocked the world by dropping atomic bombs on Japan. On September 2, 1945 the Japanese surrendered and the war was finally over. I can only imagine how my father and every other soldier must have felt to know they were finally going home. Not long after he returned, Dad once again traded in his rifle and combat boots for his fiddle and a Golden West Cowboy uniform.

In Pee Wee King's own words, his return to the band helped to create the band's golden age. While my dad was serving in the Army, Pee Wee tried out several lead vocalists, including Eddy Arnold, but felt that nobody represented the sound of the Golden West Cowboys like Redd Stewart. Eddy Arnold, the band's lead vocalist, had gone out on his own, so my dad took over the role.

From this point forward, the talents, skills, and partnership of Pee Wee and Redd began to pioneer new territory in Country music. For the next two years the Golden West Cowboys remained members of the Grand Ole Opry. During this time they brought many changes, including new instruments, new music, flashy outfits, organization and showmanship unfamiliar to the Opry.

But change didn't come easy with the Solemn Old Judge! Every time Pee Wee and the band would bring new things to the stage, the Judge would lecture Pee Wee afterwards.

In the beginning, the band stood out like a sore thumb against all the other Hillbilly performers. It took Pee Wee a while to convince the old Judge that change was inevitable and he had to keep up with the times.

When they first started out, the band wore simple matching

cowboy outfits. As time went by, their clothes began to get fancier and fancier. They started having their outfits, called Nudie suits, made in Hollywood by Nudie Cohen. Mr. Nudie was responsible for making some of the clothing for the Hollywood stars. He later made suits for all the big Country acts, even Elvis Presley.

Obviously, these outfits drew a sharp contrast to the bib overalls and checkered shirts worn by most of the other performers. Most of them, being farmers during the week, lacked the experience of the Golden West Cowboys. The band's music was extremely polished and versatile. They could play just about any style you wanted, from Western Swing, Polkas, Waltzes, Ballads and more.

The combination of Pee Wee's business skills, forward thinking, and bigger-than-life personality, along with Dad's incredible voice, musical talent and songwriting skills, they created a team that couldn't be stopped.

They were innovators and always seemed ten years ahead of their time. They brought to the stage trumpets, drums, electric guitars, the accordion and new styles of music, such as Western Swing. Some say that Pee Wee and his band electrified the Opry.

The Golden West Cowboys became a launching pad for a lot of the performers of that day. Pee Wee and my dad always encouraged band members and performers who wanted to break out on their own, and never stood in their way. A good example of this would be Jan Howard. This is what she wrote:

"One of the first shows I ever worked after moving to Nashville from California was in Grand Rapids, MI with Pee Wee King & Redd Stewart. I was petrified with stage fright, but when I handed them the charts to my songs, they said, 'You're gonna be a pro' . . . what a compliment! They never forgot that, and I never forgot their kindness to a newcomer."

During their ten years on the Grand Ole Opry, Pee Wee and his band performed with many Country music pioneers such as Uncle Dave Macon, the Delmore Brothers, Roy Acuff, Minnie Pearl, Grandpa Jones, Hank Williams, DeFord Bailey, Ernest Tubb,

Cowboy Copas, Hawkshaw Hawkins, and the list goes on. The Golden West Cowboys became a stepping-stone for many of these talented performers.

Forging Ahead

Bicycling

By now you're probably thinking my dad, Pee Wee and the band are superstars and living high on the hog, but it was quite the opposite. Remember, we're talking about the 1940s. No fancy planes, million-dollar tour buses, tractor trailers, fancy hotels, fine-dining or backstage catering. These were tough times to be in the music business.

The Grand Ole Opry only ran on Saturday nights, and the pay left a lot to be desired. To make enough money to survive, performers had to work all over the country, which made it tough to get back to Nashville to do the Opry every week.

During the week they would bounce from one small town to the next, sometimes doing two or three shows in one location. This is where the term bicycling came from. They said it felt like they were riding a bicycle racing back and forth to the shows. The 1940s lacked the road systems we have today, so bands traveled on the back roads, sometimes on dirt and gravel.

They would pack musicians into cars and trucks, often so full they had a bass fiddle sticking out the window. Keep in mind, these vehicles had no air-conditioning and there weren't any gas stations along the way. My dad said they had more flat tires than he could count, and cars broke down almost weekly.

They slept and ate in dives, all for paychecks that barely covered their bills. One time Dad said he was traveling over sixty thousand miles a year, and started feeling like he was a part of the car. He had been in every state in the United States, except Alaska at least twice. If you were a musician during this time, it was not for the money, but because you loved it.

The Grand Ole Opry wasn't much better. The Ryman Auditorium

in those days was not like the venues where Country musicians perform today. Two small areas served as dressing rooms, one for women and one for the men, and two washroom areas were used by as many as 200 performers a night. The Ryman had no air-conditioning, and during summer, temperatures could reach close to 100 degrees.

There was no lounge for performers to gather, so they would all meet out back in the alley and go to a nearby bar to relax between shows. That alleyway became a launching pad for many musicians. Performers trying to make it in the music industry would wait out back until the stars and managers came out and play their songs in hopes of getting discovered.

As the story goes, the Everly Brothers were discovered out behind the Grand Ole Opry. My dad was one of the people to encourage them.

In 1960, Tootsie Bess opened up what is now called Tootsie's Orchid Lounge. At first she called the establishment Mom's. Tootsie had been a performer herself and had a big heart for all Opry musicians. She was known to slip money into the pockets of those in need. Tootsie credits a painter with naming her lounge. She came in one day to discover he had painted her place orchid, thus the name, Tootsie's Orchid Lounge.

From the back door of the Ryman, Tootsie's back door entrance was right across the alley. This became the destination where performers went to hang out and relax between shows. Over the years, the walls became filled with pictures of all the stars who performed on the Opry and became known as the Wall of Fame.

Many musicians were discovered in Tootsie's lounge, one being Willie Nelson. Tootsie loved all her customers, but I've been told by more than one that if you got out of line, she would stick you with a hatpin! Charlie Pride was the musician who gave her the famous jeweled hatpin.

During the last few years when Pee Wee and the band were on the Opry, tent shows were extremely popular. They put together a

Grand Ole Opry Tent Show and traveled all around the south. This was extremely hard work and very time consuming. The operation required a special crew to erect the tents and tear them down so they could move to the next town.

Sometimes the performers would make money, but often didn't even make their expenses. They tried to do the shows up north, but that turned out to be a disaster, since the Opry was not as well known there.

Travel accommodations were horrific at best. These musicians stayed in boarding houses and tourist cabins, such as the famous teepee cottages in Horse Cave, Kentucky. They would stay any-where they could find inexpensive rooms. Most of these were like the bed & breakfasts of today. Sometimes the food was good, but other times not so much. Once motels became popular and more restaurants became available, the accommodations improved.

In the 1940s money was extremely tight, so performers had to eat the cheapest things on the menu. My Uncle Slim, Redd's brother, once told the story about the two of them heading over to a restaurant to eat.

Slim said to my dad, "It's chilly out here."

My dad responded, "If I know anything, it's chili every day!" Chili was the cheapest thing on the menu, and they ate quite a bit of it!

Redd and Jean get married with Don Davis as Limousine Driver
and Pee Wee and Lydia King

Ma Upchurch's Boarding House   Redd with his first born, Lydia

Redd Gets Married

In the late 1940s, a cozy little restaurant called the Blue Boar Cafeteria lay in the heart of Louisville, Kentucky. It served delicious buffet-style food and provided a popular social gathering for all the locals. One of the waitresses there was named Jean—Jeannie to all her friends. This pretty, energetic and headstrong young lady was trying to make it on her own during the war.

Around this time, my Uncle Gene went in to get some lunch at the Blue Boar, and happened to run into this friendly little waitress. I'll explain more about Gene's role in this part of the story in a moment.

Now, when Redd met Jean for the very first time, it was love at first sight. It didn't take very long until wedding bells were ringing. They married on June 16, 1946 in Nashville, Tennessee in a simple wedding with Pee Wee as the best man. His wife Lydia was the matron of honor, and Don Davis, a member of Pee Wee's band, played the role of limousine driver.

The so-called limousine was actually one of the band's travel vehicles with Pee Wee King & the Golden West Cowboys written on the fender—so much for a fancy wedding. After they married, Redd and Jeannie rented a house directly across the street from Ma Upchurch's Boarding House on Boscobel Street in East Nashville's Edgefield neighborhood.

It's only fitting that I stop to describe Ma Upchurch—a strong Christian woman who loved Hillbilly music. She and her husband lived in a big stone house in east Nashville that became a part of Country music history. It's estimated that over time more than two thousand struggling Hillbilly musicians stayed at their boarding house. Ma's home eventually became known as Hillbilly Heaven.

Before her husband passed away in 1947, Ma didn't take very many boarders. Shorty Boyd, also a member of Pee Wee's band, was the first one to talk her into letting him stay there.

The house was very large, with five bedrooms and one bathroom, a perfect setting for a boarding house. The boarders paid only $7.00 a week, plus 85 cents for dinner and 75 cents for breakfast. This affordable price attracted many musicians, and over the years Ma's home became a temporary home for thousands of young performers trying for a spot on the Opry. My dad stayed there, rooming with Grandpa Jones.

This all took place before Pa Upchurch passed away. After he died, Don Davis convinced Ma to begin taking on more boarders because so many musicians needed a place to stay. Being a widow now, she needed the added income to make ends meet.

It made good sense for my mom and dad to rent the house across the street, because Dad knew Ma and Pa Upchurch very well. Not long after my parents married, they brought a new addition into the family. Her name was Lydia, named after Pee Wee's wife.

As we grew up, my siblings and I knew Pee Wee and Lydia as Uncle Pee Wee and Aunt Lydia. It wasn't until I was older that I found out they were actually our Godparents. Despite my new revelation, my brother, sister and I still called them aunt and uncle, and we always will.

Pa Upchurch became very attached to baby Lydia and would play with her for hours. She would throw toys out of her playpen to him and he would throw them back. She would laugh for hours. Family members have told me Pa was devastated when our family left Nashville and moved back to Louisville.

"Tennessee Waltz" original manuscript

The *Tennessee Waltz* was written in 1946 and has become one of the biggest hits of all time. Despite the song's simplicity, it has been recorded and performed by hundreds of artists in every music genre imaginable. Very few songs even come close to what this song has accomplished.

Every time I listen, it amazes me that such a simple tune could become this popular. My dad always told me when I started writing my own songs to keep it simple, always tell a story, and you can never go wrong with a love song. The *Tennessee Waltz* is obviously proof of that!

Now for the true story of its creation. Very few people know that the *Tennessee Waltz* story actually happened to real characters. So, let's step back in time to the Blue Boar Cafeteria and that pretty little waitress named Jeannie (my mom.)

Remember I mentioned the role my Uncle Gene played? When Jeannie and my Uncle Gene met, they began dating and eventually fell in love.

This is how the story goes, as told to me years ago by my mom, and confirmed by other family members. At the time, my dad, Pee Wee and the band were still performing at the Grand Ole Opry and needed a bass player. They called my Uncle Gene, who just happened to play stand up bass, to come to Nashville and join the Opry.

This was an opportunity of a lifetime, so Gene convinced Jeannie to go to Nashville with him. But then, my uncle made the big mistake of introducing my mom to my dad. The lyrics of the song say this introduction occurred at a dance, but I'm not quite sure that's the way it went down.

For the life of me I don't ever remember my dad being a dancer, but he was young and cocky at this time, so anything is possible. No one has ever told me exactly where this introduction occurred. I can only assume that placing it at a dance was done to enhance the song, but I could be wrong.

As I stated before, it was love at first sight for my parents. I can almost feel your mental wheels turning as you put the pieces of this puzzle together!

I was told that unbeknownst to Gene, my mom and dad began dating. Eventually they revealed to my uncle their love and their intention to get married. As you can imagine, this didn't go over too well with Gene. I've been told that he and Dad barely spoke to one another for a whole year. This had to have been extremely difficult since they were both in the same band and traveled together every day.

When you read accounts, of which there are many, about my dad and Pee Wee writing the *Tennessee Waltz*, this is the part they leave out, for obvious reasons. My dad was a great man of faith, and right before Pee Wee hired him, he was considering going into the ministry. This was something he didn't want to reveal, so he never told this part of the story.

In every account you will hear how my dad was an avid cigar smoker and always kept a large box of matches in the glove box. When he and Pee Wee were returning from a performance in Henderson, Texas, they crossed over into Tennessee and heard Bill Monroe's song "Kentucky Waltz" on WSM's Grand Ole Opry.

Pee Wee turned to my dad and said, "You were born in Tennessee, so how come you've never written a song about your home state?" My dad responded, "We'll take care of that right now." Told you he was cocky!

My dad and Pee Wee always drove together in the luggage truck away from the others so they could think and write songs. Dad was behind the wheel when Pee Wee challenged him to write the song, so they switched places. Dad pulled out that matchbox, threw the matches out the window, tore open the box and began to scribble the words to the *Tennessee Waltz*.

It had not been long since Mom and Dad got married and the whole event was still fresh in his mind, so he wrote from his heart. If you by chance have never heard this recording, now would be a good time to listen. If you know the song, the next time you hear it you will be aware of the characters' identity—my mom, Dad and my Uncle Gene.

Upon returning home to Nashville, Dad transcribed what he had written onto manuscript paper and penciled in the notes. This was the original manuscript that was presented to Fred Rose, founder of Acuff/Rose Publishing, Inc. In this original copy, Dad drew a line through the verse, *"Oh the Tennessee Waltz, Oh the Tennessee Waltz"* and changed it to *"I Remember the Night and the Tennessee Waltz,"* a recommendation from Fred Rose.

After my dad's death, my family discovered this manuscript in his home. We all agreed that this historic piece deserved to be preserved in a special place for all to see and enjoy, so we started looking for a permanent home for this manuscript. Senator Lamar Alexander of Tennessee and a group of other people offered to purchase it from us with the intent of donating it to the University of Tennessee.

When Senator Alexander presented the manuscript to the University of Tennessee in 2013, he declared, "Finding the original manuscript of the *Tennessee Waltz* was like finding the Magna Carta of Country music."

Tennessee Waltz

By REDD STEWART and PEE WEE KING

RECORDED BY PATTI PAGE FOR MERCURY RECORDS

Featured by
PATTI PAGE

PUBLISHED BY

Acuff-Rose PUBLICATIONS
2510 FRANKLIN ROAD
NASHVILLE 4, TENNESSEE

MADE IN U.S.A.

Patti Page records "The Tennessee Waltz"

To make extra money in the early years, my dad tried to sell songs he had written that he felt had little potential. He did this backstage at the Opry. He tried to sell his *Tennessee Waltz* to many artists, including Cowboy Copas, but they all turned him down.

I can only assume he didn't think the *Tennessee Waltz* had enough commercial appeal. After all, it was a very simple song, and most people thought there were too many waltzes already out there.

Dad tucked the manuscript in his fiddle case for about six months. The band eventually began to sing it on radio shows, and eventually several other artists recorded it. In 1948 my dad and Pee Wee recorded the song, and it did very well on the charts for a short period of time. Eventually it faded away, but in 1951 everything changed.

One artist who recorded the *Tennessee Waltz* before my dad and Pee Wee was an R&B artist named Erskine Hawkins on Coral Records. In 1950 a young lady by the name of Carol Ann Fowler from Oklahoma was becoming very popular on the Mercury label. Her stage name was Patti Page.

Harry Rosen, a distributor for Mercury Records, told the Eastern vice president that he would order 45,000 copies if Patti Page would record an R&B song, "Boogie Woogie Santa Claus. "This preorder would almost guarantee a success. So, in 1951 they set up a recording session, but needed something to put on the B side of the record.

Patti's manager Jack Rael bumped into Jerry Wexlar, who reviewed records for Billboard Magazine. He told her manager that he had received a song by Erskine Hawkins, a country song titled the *Tennessee Waltz*. He declared, "If a pop artist got a hold of this and recorded it, it could be a smash hit."

Patti's manager got a copy of the song, played it for her, and they decided to make it the B side of the record. Patti's record company wanted to focus on the Christmas song, so it's very likely they picked the *Tennessee Waltz* because it was good enough to protect her image, but not strong enough to compete with *Boogie Woogie Santa Claus*.

So much for logic.

The results of the recording went beyond anyone's expectations. The hit side turned out to be *Tennessee Waltz*! Patti's recording spent 13 weeks at No. 1 and reached No. 2 on the Country chart. At last count, the recording has sold well over ten million copies, the largest selling record by a female artist in recording history.

Because of this overwhelming success, many big artists began to record covers of Patti's version. This was the beginning of becoming one of the greatest songs ever written.

The Impact of *Tennessee Waltz*

In 2003 when my dad passed away, my wife Sharon and I decided to build a tribute website in his honor. Once the website was built, Sharon took over the daunting task of maintaining and continually adding new content. She thought it would be of interest to readers to add a section called 'Various Versions of *Tennessee Waltz*,' and began researching as many recordings of the song as she could find.

She put the artist's name, the album cover and a link to the MP3 of their recording on the page. After discovering over 200 different recordings, she finally gave up because there just was not enough space on the website. This section only scratches the surface of the recordings out there. Sharon also researches all new YouTube versions of this song annually, and is constantly amazed at how many new and older artists, either pro or amateur, have recorded the song, which appears to be immortal.

Here is a very small sample of the artists who have recorded the *Tennessee Waltz* through the years: Patti Page, Jean Shepard, Emmylou Harris, Jerry Lee Lewis, Hank Williams, Hank Williams, Jr., Anne Murray, Faron Young, Elvis Presley, Connie Francis, Patsy Cline, Jim Reeves, Les Paul & Mary Ford, Norah Jones, Cowboy Copas, Tennessee Ernie Ford, Eddy Arnold, Dean Martin, Leonard Cohen, Tom Jones, Pam Tillis, Roy Acuff, Ernest Tubb, Bonnie Rait, Kitty Wells, Sam Cooke, Otis Redding, Floyd Cramer, Lacy J. Dalton, Cristy Lane, Ella Fitzgerald, Daniel O'Donnell, Tommy Emmanuel, Billy Vaughn, Doc Severinsen—and the list goes on!

When I began writing my own songs, my dad told me never

to prejudge your music, advice I have followed over the years. He told me that you never know how the public is going to react to a song. He never in a million years thought the *Tennessee Waltz* would become so successful. He said he believed many of his hits did not have much potential.

To be honest, when listening to the *Tennessee Waltz*, I'm surprised that such a simple song has grown so popular. The key was being recorded at the right time by the right people.

As time goes on, the list of Top 10 best songs ever written keeps changing. One year "Blue Moon" might be considered No. 1, the next year it could be "Moon River" or "Hey Jude," but one thing is for sure: the *Tennessee Waltz* almost always makes this list. Its popularity is global and it has been recorded and performed in just about every music genre you can imagine.

We call it the immortal *Tennessee Waltz*. At one point, Patti Page's recording held the record as the best selling song by a female artist. It has also won numerous BMI airplay awards, along with many others.

Over the years we have heard hundreds of testimonies and stories of what the song has meant to people. It has been played from weddings to funerals to nursing homes, every place imaginable. The following are examples of some of the stories we have been told:

"Having played steel guitar in country bands for over 40 years, I was familiar with and am an admirer of Redd and Pee Wee. They were better than anything we have today. If I had a nickel for every time I've played *Tennessee Waltz*, I could buy that bass boat I've always wanted."

~Harry Marlin, Steel Guitarist, Brownwood, Texas

"Mama played piano and taught me the *Tennessee Waltz* when I was just a toddler. I'm now on the road and play it every night! She said, 'Don't give up, pray, have faith, keep a positive mental attitude and love each other.'"

~Anthony John Robertson, Spring City, Tennessee

"The *Tennessee Waltz* was the first song I remember my mother singing to me. I never knew who wrote it. I wish I could say thanks to Redd in person. I'll love that song until the day I join him."

~Kim Herman, Friendswood, Texas

"I want you to know that I absolutely *love* his songs and my personal favorite, and one that I hope to include on my album some day is *Tennessee Waltz*. I used to sing it for a dear old friend of mine. He was 85 years old and it was his favorite song because it brought back memories of his dearly departed wife. We cried many times together when I sang that beautiful song to him. I actually sang for him for about an hour and a half, and two hours later he passed on. It is a good memory, and I know the song gave him release. It is a blessing to have someone who was so talented and left us with art like Redd did."

~Joanne Myrol. Alberta, Canada

"I have been '*Tennessee Waltz*ing' in Nashville and Country music as a songwriter for nearly 36 years, and it is forerunners like Redd and Pee Wee that paved the way for grateful songwriters like myself."

~Charlie Craig, Mt. Juliet, Tennessee

"Redd was indeed a wonderful songwriter and artist. *Tennessee Waltz* will live on forever. We never do a show without singing it. It's always requested."

~Paul & Helen Mateki, Ft. Worth, Texas

"I've always said there is one thing you can count on, *Tennessee Waltz* was, is and will continue to be the ultimate Country song. We all can feel that little tug on our heartstrings within the first couple of notes."

~Nancy, Alabama

"Redd Stewart was surely one of the best writers in the Country music field (and more) so that it's great that you did this very fine website in his tribute. I never had the luck to meet him, but I listen to Country music for so many years, and the *Tennessee Waltz* is without any doubt, one of the most famous and beautiful songs in that field!"

~Massimo Ferro, Alessandria, Italy

"Redd Stewart is one of my most requested Classic Country music artists across the years, and his *Tennessee Waltz* is today nearly an evergreen in the country music."

~Dann Hansen, Denmark

"I have always loved Redd's music. I used to work at ShoBud guitar company in Nashville and have been in many bands over the years. I have sung *Tennessee Waltz* a couple of thousand times. What a monster song! We need more Country music like that."

~Flash Gordon, Springfield, Tennessee

"I am a 10-year old Country singer, and I really enjoy listening to Redd's songs, especially *Tennessee Waltz*. I would love to have a songwriter with his talent in my corner."

~Jourdan Irene, Mt. Bethel, Pennsylvania

It is almost impossible to determine just how many recordings of *Tennessee Waltz* have been sold. Patti Page's recording alone has sold well over 10 million copies. It has been recorded by hundreds of other artists—you do the math.

Ingrained in many people's minds, this song stirs up many memories and has such a powerful meaning to so many. Not many songs become a part of history, but *Tennessee Waltz* has done just that. I want to take just a minute to shine a spotlight on some of the previous and current events that have put *Tennessee Waltz* on the center stage.

1. February 17, 1965—Governor Frank Clement officially proclaimed *Tennessee Waltz* the Tennessee state song.

2. The University of Tennessee Pride of the Southland Band & The Baylor University Golden Wave band both play *Tennessee Waltz* after every football game.

3. Pat Summit was an American women's college basketball head coach of the University of Tennessee Lady Vols basketball team. Her favorite song was *Tennessee Waltz*. To honor her many accomplishments, the bells at the University of Tennessee's Ayres Hall played the *Tennessee Waltz* after her death.

4. In 2013 Redd's original manuscript of *Tennessee Waltz* was given to the University of Tennessee's Natalie L. Haslam Music Center, where it hangs today.

"The right home for the songwriters' original manuscript of the state song that has become the most popular song in the history of Country music is the Natalie L. Haslam Music Center at our state university," US Senator Lamar Alexander said. "According to music historian Robert K. Oermann, finding this historic document is 'like finding the Magna Carta of country music.'"

5. Bicentennial Capitol Mall State Park, also known as the Bicentennial Mall, is an urban state park in downtown Nashville, Tennessee. The northern end of the park features the Court of Three Stars, a circular plaza made of red, white, and blue granite representing the three Grand Divisions of Tennessee. Surrounding the plaza, 50 columns containing a 95-bell carillon represent the state's ninety-five counties and its musical legacy. The carillon automatically plays portions of the *Tennessee Waltz* every quarter hour, completing the entire song on the hour.

6. Kelly Clarkson performed *Tennessee Waltz* at the 2013 Grammy Awards as part of a tribute to Patti Page after her death.

7. In 2009 The Nashville Music Garden located at the Walk of Fame Park between Fourth and Fifth Avenues in front of the Country Music Hall of Fame in downtown Nashville, placed a

Tennessee Waltz rose in the garden. In 2005 the *Tennessee Waltz* miniature pink-blend rose was created by Whit Wells.

8. *Tennessee Waltz* was awarded BMI's 3,000,000 Airplay Award. This prestigious honor is shared with Barry Manilow's, "I Write The Songs," Frank Sinatra's "My Way," Hank Williams', "Your Cheatin' Heart," Elvis Presley's "Love Me Tender" and Roger Miller's "King of the Road."

9. Acuff-Rose Song Catalog—Grand Ole Opry star Roy Acuff and songwriter-musician Fred Rose established the company in 1942, a time when Nashville had virtually no publishing activity in Country music. It didn't take long for the business to catch on. Among early Acuff-Rose treasures was *Tennessee Waltz*, the company's first major pop hit by Patti Page in 1950.

10. The Music City Drum and Bugle Corps, a World Class competitive junior drum and bugle corps, is based in Nashville Tennessee and a member corps of Drum Corps International Open Class. The *Tennessee Waltz* is the Music City Corps' song.

11. In 2005, *Tennessee Waltz* Parkway was named in Ashland City, Tennessee in honor of Redd Stewart, born in Ashland City.

12. As of 1974, *Tennessee Waltz* was the largest selling song ever in Japan. In Japanese schools, the song is a standard taught in all music programs.

13. The American Queen Cruise Ship steamed into its home port of Memphis in 2012. The 436-passenger ship, with a 174-person crew, docked in the city for the first time since a previous owner pulled it out of service in 2008. Passengers sipped mimosas and bloody Marys on the ship's forward deck, while Captain John Sutton ordered the ship's whistle blown in welcome, and the calliope played *Tennessee Waltz* and "Rocky Top."

14. In 2015, Crowned Heads created a cigar named *Tennessee Waltz*. "It was the song that was playing in the dance hall when my maternal grandfather met my grandmother. I vividly recall him whistling that tune throughout my childhood. It's a song that was made popular in 1950 by Patti Page, and has been recorded by everyone from Sam Cooke to Otis Redding to Norah Jones.

"The state of Tennessee is also near and dear to my heart. I met my wife here, my family is here, and of course, Crowned Heads is headquartered here in Nashville. Crowned Heads owes a great deal to the people of Tennessee for their support from the very beginning. And so it is with a sincere spirit of gratitude that we present *Tennessee Waltz*."

15. In 2016, the lights of the Tennessee State Capitol were softly dimmed for the Twenty-fourth annual *A Tennessee Waltz*. And for the fourteenth consecutive year, Jack Daniel's Distillery presented the black-tie benefit for the Tennessee State Museum.

Life After the Grand Ole Opry

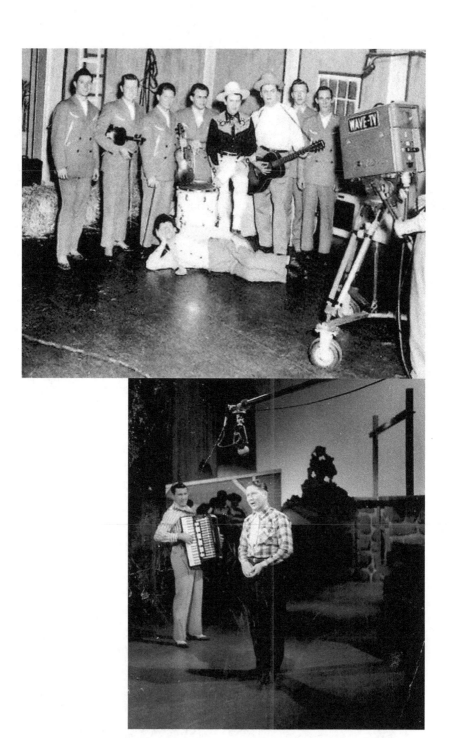

Pee Wee and the Band Leave the Grand Ole Opry

In 1947 J.L. Frank and his wife were in a car accident in Louisville, Kentucky. Both of them had to be hospitalized, so Pee Wee took some time off to visit them. Right after J.L. got out of the hospital, he talked to the general manager of WAVE-TV in Louisville to see about Pee Wee and the band doing a television show there. The manager was very interested, so plans were made to produce a show of Pee Wee and the boys.

Pee Wee believed that the future was in TV, but was very reluctant to leave the Grand Ole Opry for good. In Nashville, he talked with the top brass of National Life & Casualty Company, the owners of the Opry and WSM radio. This station had 50,000 watts of power, but WAVE-TV became operational at only 20,000 watts.

This was very concerning to Pee Wee because they wouldn't be able to reach as large an audience as WSM radio could. He asked the top brass if they would be interested in bringing TV to Nashville, but they were completely opposed and felt TV was just a passing fad. They also told him that if he went into TV and flopped, he could return to the Grand Ole Opry. Pee Wee was ecstatic because he had watched many leave the Opry who had not been able to return.

In October of 1947 the band made the move to Louisville, and by Thanksgiving were already recording television shows. WAVE-TV had five buyers waiting to purchase them. Many people asked Pee Wee why they had left the Opry. His response was that after ten years and traveling all over the country, including seven foreign countries, he and the band members were tired and ready for a break.

Doing the TV shows, radio shows and a lot fewer live performances allowed them to have more of a family life and settle down. The move to TV proved to be a big success.

In the beginning, the move to Louisville was supposed to be about slowing down, but once my dad and Pee Wee started doing television, they got the bug and the race was on! Times were changing and so was music. Pee Wee and my dad were always keen on changing with the times.

Their television shows began to feature Country artists as well as some Pop artists. Even their writing style began to change. Once they established the show at WAVE-TV, they expanded into Cleveland, Ohio with a 26-week show on WEWS-TV, Cleveland.

In the early 1950s it was a big deal for an artist to have one television show, but to have two was unheard of. Not only did Pee Wee and Dad have these two shows, they didn't stop there. By 1955 they were doing four television shows aired on six different stations. Their popularity had grown like wild fire.

Television put my dad out there in the spotlight more than anything else they had ever done. During this period he and Pee Wee were becoming an inseparable team.

Every time I listen to my dad sing, I am amazed at his vocal talent. His range was incredible, with a voice as smooth as glass. He sounded like no one else. This became more and more evident as many reviews appeared in billboards and magazines about the recordings, live performances, and television shows. As years passed, they began to market the shows as Pee Wee King & His Golden West Cowboys, featuring Redd Stewart.

However, television was not without its problems. Fans no longer were buying records as much because they could see bands on television. This unfortunately created a drastic drop in record sales. But at the same time, the more fans watched the band on television, the more they began to request seeing live performances. Juggling live performances and recording sessions combined with four television shows became quite a feat, but one they took on full force.

Not only did they have huge success on television, but these years were also times of their biggest hits—"Bonaparte's Retreat" in 1949, Patti Page's recording of *Tennessee Waltz* in 1951, "Slow Poke," a huge success in 1951, and "You Belong to Me" in 1952. These four songs became standards and remain so to this day.

A standard song becomes so popular that it crosses over and is recorded in other music genres. The 1950s were truly golden years for my dad and Pee Wee King. No one at that time experienced nearly as much success on television.

I'd like to share a few stories we heard after my dad's death.

The first was shared by Bobby Koefer, steel guitarist & former Golden West Cowboys member:

"I was with Bob Wills before going with Pee Wee King in Louisville in early 1952. I took Roy Ayres' place when he left. I worked with Redd for exactly 3 years—1952, 1953, and 1954. I worked the radio shows over WAVE, the TV shows, recorded, and all the appearances that were made during that period.

"Redd was one of the most talented guys I ever worked with. His singing and songwriting spoke for itself. I used to be amazed at his ability sometimes in the studio when we might just be fooling around before a radio show started. He might pick up a guitar, or his fiddle, and play some great swing and improvising, and didn't even think about it. He didn't get to do that very often.

"Before I forget, here's a little trivia for you. I was talking to Bob Wills about leaving and going with Pee Wee King. Bob and his longtime vocalist, Tommy Duncan had broken up. Bob told me that he always had liked Redd Stewart's singing, and when he and Tommy had broken up, he had considered talking to Redd about going to work for him and the Texas Playboys. As far as I know, he never did follow through with his thinking. I would take that as a great compliment to Redd, regardless of whether or not Redd would have been interested."

This next story was shared by Mitchell Torok, Country music singer, songwriter, artist, author and guitarist:

"Having been around since my number one hit songs in 1953, I ran into Pee Wee King and Redd several times at the old Disc Jockey Conventions of that era—this would be in 1955–56–57—when we all tried to congregate in the old Andrew Jackson hotel here in Nashville to visit and talk to DJs, etc, and otherwise tell everyone how great were! Just kidding!

"I did play Pee Wee's TV show out of Chicago during this time also. I sang the song "Mexican Joe In The Caribbean," of course it was live TV and one thing I do remember, when I started one of the songs, I forgot which one, it was a mess, and though we did rehearse a little before the show, we had to stop a minute or two into the song and start over! It was embarrassing for both Pee Wee and I, but we laughed and joked our way through it!

"Pee Wee and Redd were great songwriters, and their music catalog shows that. I've always admired them both. When I was growing up, "Slow Poke" was big with me."

"Redd Stewart was a marvelous talent and a kind and gentle man. I toured with him a bit and always enjoyed welcoming him and Pee Wee King to the Grand Ole Opry. You'd be amazed at how many Opry stars considered Redd to be one of their favorite Country music singers. I'm glad you folks are keeping his music and memory alive."

~Bill Anderson (Whisperin' Bill, Grand Ole Opry Legend)

"I played steel guitar with Redd for over eight years in Pee Wee King's band, starting in 1946 at the Grand Ole Opry and continuing through 1954 on WAVE-TV in Louisville, KY. I left the business as a profession for 42 years and recently retired, resuming music as a hobby.

"To me, Redd was the glue that held the Golden West Cowboys together into a tight musical unit. Redd was a great musician and songwriter, and above all, was a friend and gentleman. I miss him."

~Roy Ayres, former Golden West Cowboys member

"As a boy I watched Redd and brother Gene perform with Pee Wee King on our local TV station. They all were rhinestone cowboys to me. I wanted to be just like 'em when I got older - love the music, the excitement of the fans. Well, my dreams came true! Later I became an entertainer, also. Got the chance to meet Redd, and even played with Gene and Pee Wee years later. They all have a special place in my memories and my heart."

~Louie Knight (aka King Louie)

"There are so many wonderful stories that I could tell everyone, because Redd Stewart and Pee Wee King were like fathers to me. They nurtured my musical career with advice and support, and I loved them both very much. These people have been so instrumental in what I have done in my life and what I have accomplished in Country music.

"Redd always told me to be honest, keep my integrity and my faith, and to keep my friends close by me. Both him and Pee Wee are still in my heart and my mind."

~Marty Martel, President R.O.P.E.

"I enjoyed Redd and Pee Wee's music. I played in a lead off band for them at a concert in Amsterdam, New York back in the 1960s, also was on stage with Willie Nelson when he was starting out. You have really put together a well-deserved website of love and admiration for a Western Swing & Country music legend that was a tremendous songwriter, musician and one of the greatest voices that this world will ever know!

"It is my pleasure to play lots of Redd's material, both as a vocalist with the great Pee Wee King band, or his own recordings on my *Swingin' West* radio show. In addition, I really enjoy playing other artists also doing Redd's wonderful compositions. Redd has been an integral part of my *Swingin' West* programming since the show started back in 1980, and he will always be."

~Mike Gross, D.J., Fairfield, Connecticut

Chicago, August 1, 1942   Vol. 9—No. 15

ALL RECORDING STOPS TODAY

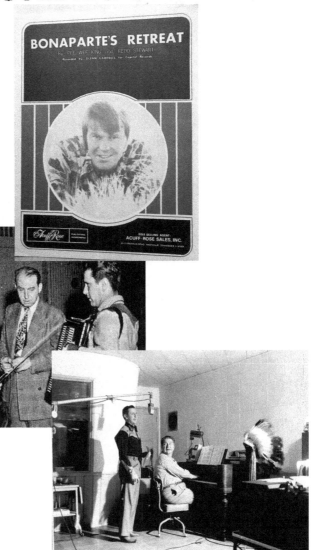

The Recording Bans

In 1947, all the musicians in the musician's union were getting ready for the second recording ban. The first ban was from 1942 until 1944. James C. Petrillo, president of the Musician's Union (American Federation of Musicians) did not like the fact that work for union musicians was shrinking. He felt that recordings were causing the lack of work. A recording could be played time and again, but musicians would only get paid for the time it was recorded, not for the many times it would be played afterwards.

To try to correct this, he implemented a recording ban for all union musicians. The second union ban was to start January 1, 1948. Musicians scrambled to set up sessions and record as many songs as they possibly could before the ban went into place.

Once the second recording ban was lifted, my dad and Pee Wee headed to the studio for a long-awaited recording session. Their recording of *Tennessee Waltz* surpassed their expectations, so they wanted to capitalize on that momentum by recording a few more waltzes. Two of those were "The Waltz of the Alamo" and "Whisper Waltz." However, the best song to come out of this recording session was "Bonaparte's Retreat."

As the story goes, my dad & Pee Wee were rehearsing some square dance numbers with a boy from Texas and he showed them a recording of a Texas square dance tune called "Bonaparte's Retreat," which had sort of a Cajun beat and was a folk tune in public domain. Dad & Pee Wee took part of the melody, put a bridge or middle to it, wrote some words and reshaped the whole song, building on its folk base.

Their recording with the Golden West Cowboys had good sales, but this song didn't become a smash hit until Kay Starr did her recording. She heard the jukebox version by accident as she and her husband were driving across the country and stopped at a restaurant. She asked the owner to sell her the record, but he refused until she told him who she was. He gave it to her when she promised to send him an autographed copy of her version. (She had already made up her mind to record it.)

Through the years, this song has been covered by many artists. Later in the 1970s, Pee Wee got a phone call from Glen Campbell, who told him of the tremendous response he was getting with their version, on which he played bagpipes. He said he was thinking of releasing a single. He did, and the pride of Delight, Arkansas took the song to No. 3 in 1974. This is another example of a song crossing over into pop music and eventually becoming a standard.

In the United States, any musical works published in 1924 or earlier, in addition to those voluntarily placed in public domain, exist in the public domain. In most other countries, music generally enters the public domain 50 to 75 years after the composer's death. Any song in public domain can be recorded by anyone without paying royalties to the original writer.

Many hits through the years were originally old tunes found in public domain. A recent example of this is the song, "Ain't No Grave," which as of 2020 has become a very popular worship song.

Where did "Bonaparte's Retreat" originate? The original wordless melody existed as various fiddle tunes dating back to at least the late 1800s and probably well before that. The title of the original tune refers to Napoleon Bonaparte's disastrous retreat from Russia in 1812, which led to his downfall and finally ended the danger that he would invade England. Some 19th-century British folk songs celebrated this event.

The Golden West Cowboys performing in "Rough Tough West"

Redd singing "You Don't Need my Love Anymore" in the movie

In 1951 a young lady named Chilton Price worked as a music librarian at the radio station in Louisville, and had written some songs and decided to give them to my dad and Pee Wee to see about their potential. Dad and Pee Wee slowly worked through each one, revising some lyrics and making improvements to the melodies to create more marketable versions.

One of these was titled "Slow Poke." The band tried the song out at live shows to a very encouraging response. They decided to take it to the studio, but their attempts to record produced an emptiness and it did not sound the same as when they performed it live. They tried numerous enhancements, but only when their drummer picked up an old tempo box did everything change. Striking that tempo box with a drumstick created a tic toc sound that completely changed the song.

The recording was released on RCA Victor Records and reached the bestseller chart on *Billboard Magazine* in October 1951. It stayed on the charts for 22 weeks and peaked at No. 3. In September 1951 it reached the Country charts and lasted 31 weeks, peaking at No. 1. "Slow Poke" remained at No. 1 for 15 weeks! How many artists today can do that?

Outside the U.S., "Slow Poke" topped the Australian charts in May 1952. It also became a hit in the United Kingdom under the title "Slow Coach." This earned my dad and Pee Wee their first gold record.

My dad and Pee Wee worked on another of Chilton's songs, "You Belong to Me." This recording became a national hit in 1952 and sold more than 2 million copies. Jo Stafford recorded the most popular version, which became her biggest hit, topping the charts in both the US and the United Kingdom (the first song by a female singer to top the UK chart.)

On August 29, 1952 Dean Martin released his version, reaching No. 12 and staying on the charts for 10 weeks. In 1958 the song crossed over into rock music for the first time on the Capital album, *Gene Vincent Rocks and the Blue Caps Roll*. A later version by The Duprees also made the Billboard Top 10, reaching No. 7 in 1962. After my dad passed away, my wife Sharon spoke with one of The Duprees, and he said he would forever be grateful to Redd for that song, as it took them to the top.

Many other pop vocalists, including Patsy Cline and Bing Crosby, recorded this song. It has also appeared on many movie soundtracks. A version by Jason Wade was part of the soundtrack in the 2001 animated film *Shrek*. Rocker Tori Amos also sang the classic for the Julia Roberts film *Mona Lisa Smile* in 2003. Actress Rose McGowan sang it in the soundtrack for The Planet Terror segment of the 2007 movie, *Grindhouse*.

While onscreen, Bette Midler sings a fragment of the song (to Nick Nolte) in the 1986 comedy *Down and Out in Beverly Hills*. On February 1, 2007, a short rendition of the song was sung by 64-year-old Sherman Pore as an audition piece for the television show *American Idol*, as a tribute to his wife who had died of cancer two days before.

June 15, 1952: *The Rough, Tough West*, an American western film directed by Ray Nazarro and starring Charles Starrett, Jock Mahoney and Carolina Cotton, was released. This occurred during the last year of the *Durango Kid* film series. At this late date, the series relied on cost-cutting measures to stay within a low budget, so this film contains footage from older Starrett westerns.

For those unfamiliar with the movie or actors, Charles Starrett was an American actor best known for his starring role in the *Durango Kid* western series. Lester Burnett (aka Smiley Burnett) was an American music performer and comedic actor in western films and on radio and TV, playing sidekick to Gene Autry and Roy Rogers. American actress and singer Carolina Cotton was known as the 'Yodeling Blonde Bombshell,' the 'Girl of the Golden West,' and the 'Queen of the Range.'

This movie was my dad's claim to fame as an actor. He appeared several times as part of Pee Wee King & His Golden West Cowboys, performing in bar scenes and some outside scenes, but my favorite part is when he sings solo "You Don't Need my Love Anymore."

His voice is amazing, as always, but I have to laugh every time I see him do the little dance in the middle of the song. You can find this movie on YouTube. Just search for *The Rough Tough West* (1952). This was Dad's first and last movie, and I'm always impressed at how natural he seemed. But when I think about all the television shows he did, I realize he was already used to being in front of a camera.

When he first started with Pee Wee, he was very shy, but taking over as lead vocalist forced him into the spotlight. This was probably the best thing that ever happened in his career. Over the years he became quite the entertainer.

Time Off the Road

Redd and Jean out for an evening with friends

Our Western-Style home

Meanwhile Back at Home

This is probably a great place to tell you what life was like at home while my dad was out on the road. As you can tell, the '50s were the band's heyday, the golden years of Dad and Pee Wee's career together. They were just about as busy as you could possibly be, and their popularity was huge. This brought both of them a great financial return, and life was getting way better than during the '30s and '40s.

A few years before I was born, my dad bought a really nice house in what was and still is the best part of Louisville to rear a family. We lived in St. Mathews in the east end in a subdivision called Norbourne Estates. You may be thinking something comparable to Graceland Estates, but far from it! This was a normal suburban home in a very family-friendly neighborhood. Nothing huge, but a nice house.

At this stage, my mother probably looked like an octopus juggler with thirty balls in the air. She pretty much handled everything other than paying the bills. That was my dad's job. She had three kids, a home to care for, a yard to mow, plus a dog.

Mom was the Cub Scout den mother and highly involved in the church we attended. If anything went wrong it was on her, but she handled it like a champ! She was determined, devoted and my dad's backbone. She went out of her way to make our lives special. We had a great home, wonderful birthdays, over-the-top Christmases, and everything in between. Dad hired a lady to come in a few times a week to help with laundry and cleaning because Mom was so busy.

Our house was about as western as you can get. The living room had solid, incredibly heavy ranch oak furniture, stuff you did not want to bump into. The lamps on each side of the couch were classic ranch oak, western-style, complete with cowhide lampshades... *Yeeeehawwww!* A huge painting of cowboys gathered around a cattle drive's chuck wagon hung above the couch, complete with a large ranch oak frame.

Thankfully they toned down the 'western' a little bit in the dining room. That room had a little more traditional look.

The house had a huge basement. When you went down the open flight of steps, to the left sat a big laundry room with some storage. To the right was a large L-shaped family room with a separate room for Dad's office. In the larger part of the family room was a really nice pool table, his pride and joy. A little secret about Redd Stewart: he was one fine pool player and loved the game.

The other side of the family room housed a large upright piano where he spent a lot of time writing music. The whole basement had solid pine plank paneling, not the cheap stuff but the thick expensive kind. The basement was, of course, decorated with fine western garb. Our house was a cowboy ranch in suburbia Louisville, and the only thing missing was a rodeo in the backyard.

This was a great time in our life. We had tons of friends, money was good and it was a great time to be alive in America. Whenever my dad would come into town, he went out of his way to make things special. We were members of Woodhaven Country Club, as were many of my parents' friends. In summer, that's where you would find us.

My dad was an avid golfer and an extremely good player. The country club was where my parents could go with their friends and Dad could be normal. Us kids would have a ball in the pools, Dad would hit a couple of rounds of golf with his buddies, and Mom would hang and sunbathe with all the other wives. Doesn't get much better than that!

It seemed that all the hard work my mom and dad had endured was paying off. I really think that right about the time my mom was at her wits' end, my dad would roll in and make it all good. This was a time when patriotism was strong, the country united, the economy good and new technology changing the way we lived. In our neighborhood, neighbors didn't even lock their doors. Let's be honest here, any decade that created the '57 Chevy has got to be good, and let's not forget Rock and Roll.

I could spend days telling you stories I remember and others my family told of wonderful and funny experiences during this time, but this book can only be so long. We have handpicked some to give you a little inside view of our family. I hope you enjoy them as much as we did living them.

My dad never was much of a cigarette smoker that I remember, but he was a big cigar smoker and loved his pipes. He built up quite a fine collection and was very proud of them. I remember riding in the car when I was a kid and he would be puffing on that pipe as we rolled down the road.

I didn't have a problem with his pipe because whatever tobacco he used had a very pleasant smell, but those big nasty cigars left me carsick. Lucky for me, he smoked the pipe more than the cigars. When this next story takes place, I may have been too young to remember.

Lucky for us, after my dad died, Roy Ayres, the steel guitar player in the Golden West Cowboys, shared some great tales with us. Roy posted this one in the guest book on Dad's tribute website. This is about my dad's pipe collection, and it's a funny one.

"Now, in looking over the pictures, the one of Redd with his pipe brought to mind a funny story that you may enjoy: Redd was quite a pipe smoker, and was very proud of his collection of pipes. As you may or may not know, it takes quite a bit of smoking to 'break in' a new pipe. One that is properly broken in will have a fairly thick crust of that 'nasty' residue left in the bowl from the burning tobacco.

One day Redd got home from one of those weeks-long road trips and Jean, not understanding how guys liked their pipes broken in and cruddy, had a surprise for him. She had 'cleaned' that crud out of all of his well-broken-in pipes, thinking she was doing something great for Redd.

Of course, Redd then had to go through the process of 'breaking in' all of his pipes again. He apparently wasn't upset with her, as he laughed about it when he told the guys in the band. Incidentally, Jean was a great lady, herself. She and my first wife Shirley (deceased in '88) were good friends and visited a lot when we were on the road."

With Dad being gone so much, it was only natural that my mother would experiment with different hobbies. One of these ended up being houseplants. The following is a funny story told by my sister, Lydia about one particular houseplant my father became no fan of!

"I remember Mom taking so much pride and time with dozens of house plants when I was very young. I remember wondering why she thought so much of some green vine that looked as though it should be outside, not sitting on an end table or the coffee table.

But I particularly remember one that she had so tenderly placed on the top of our television set. The televisions were so different then—this was a 'floor model' that was nearly the size of a chair. It's not that the screen was so large, but the cabinet took up so much room and made it quite large.

Mom had been told that she could grow a very nice plant by rooting a sweet potato and then planting it. She had followed all the instructions and finally had the beginnings of a plant. She placed the young plant on top of the television so that it would have plenty of space to grow and spread out.

I suppose the heat from the television and her constant attention agreed with the plant as it began to grow in leaps and bounds. It wasn't long until the entire top of the TV was covered with the vine. She began to wind it around and around until it began to hang over the side of the TV.

At this time, as usual, Daddy was traveling much of the time and at first he was amused with her trial at the plant growing, but each time he would come home from a trip, he would remark at just how big it was getting. Time after time he would acknowledge what a 'green thumb' Mom had and would just look at the forest growing so fast on its display.

But as the months went by, his comments changed from 'looks nice' to 'Just how big are you going to let that thing get?' Or 'Aren't you ever going to trim it?' The television was near the front door and you had to pass it every time you went in or out. Finally, one day as he came in from a long trip his remarks turned to, 'Jean! You have to do something with that plant. I feel like it is going to grab me and choke me.'

In the house at Norbourne Estates, on the left side of the living room was a door that led to the hallway and all the bedrooms. Right beside the door in the hallway stood a large closet where my dad kept all of his stage clothes, and it was pretty much off limits to us kids.

It really wasn't a big deal to me because I was probably too young to realize the significance of what he kept in that closet. For my sister Lydia, on the other hand, who was seven years older than me, the closet became a magical place. This is the story she tells about that special closet.

"There was a small closet off the hallway of our house that I thought to be nearly magical. It held all the clothes that Daddy would wear whenever he was entertaining. He called it "wardrobe." It didn't matter to me what he called it, but it was the suits and shirts, the neckerchiefs and hats, and of course his boots. He never wore any of these things unless he was going to perform. They were special and not for every day.

All the shirts had piping and trim on the collar and around the front. The jackets were made special to match the pants. He had several suits made by Nudie, the man who created suits for all the big stars in Nashville.

I remember the smell that came from that closet whenever you would open it up. All of his neckerchiefs hung on a tie rack on the inside of the door. There were white ones, gold ones, silver ones, and many other colors. A couple of them even had polka dots or horse's heads as the design. I suppose the neckerchief was to serve as a symbol of cowboys in the old west that wore them to cover their face during dust storms, to keep their neck warm on a cool night on the prairie, or for some of the not-so-reputable ones, to hide their face when they were holding up the stage or a bank.

But there is a real difference between the scarves of yesterday's cowboys and the ones Daddy used. The original neckerchiefs were usually just square pieces of material that they tied around their neck. But his were sewn together in the middle so they could be easily tied and would lay flat around the neck. I was always fascinated by them as it seemed to be the finishing touch to his wardrobe—the next to the last thing he would put on.

The hats always were kept in a special box so that the top crease and the sides would stay in a certain position. Each musician had their own style of cowboy hats. Some artists wore them curled a lot in the front and then some almost wore them flat, and the crease in the top was something special, too. Daddy liked his so that he could use just two fingers and his thumb to pick up his hat and put it on his head.

He always kept his boots in the closet too. He had a small foot for a man—about a 7 or 7 ½. He always had a hard time finding boots that he liked and that fit him, but what wonderful boots he had! They were always tooled or had multiple colored inlays. He had a pair of white, black, brown and blue. Those were my favorite and they had two or three shades of blue, white and cream with a real fancy design. I used to try to walk in them but with that heel, my foot always slid down into the toe, and I ended up having to drag my feet just to be able to walk. The top of the boots came up past my knees when I was younger, and it always served as a reminder of just how far I had to go to be a 'grown up.'

Now that I have reached this stage of my life, I wish I had one of Daddy's neckerchiefs—just to tie around my neck from time to time. I would love those waves of wonderful sweet memories once again that I felt whenever I would open that closet in the hallway."

A lot of the things I've written about so far were learned long after my childhood. An example of that is how my grandfather would always have family and friends over to the house and pull all the kids out to perform for everyone. From what I've been told, they were quite the rowdy bunch!

All of the kids carried the family tradition into their own lives and families. With so many of them playing on the road, it wasn't often that everyone would be in town at the same time. But when they were home, they took full advantage of it.

My Aunt Juanita's house, whom we all called Aunt Sissy, seemed to be the main hangout for this wild crew, all of them comedians who loved to pull pranks. Jam sessions were always the main event. There was a big meal preparation, plenty of jokes and laughter and just an all-around great time.

After the meal, the instruments all came out. Fiddles, guitars, banjos, upright bass, and numerous other instruments were scattered all over the place. Everything started out in that magical tuning session, trying to tune their instruments at the same time. Once the tuning session ended, the music would start. I'm sure you could hear it from five blocks away, and everybody knew the Stewarts were all in town.

The holidays were always a big deal, but it was hard to get everybody in town at the same time. My dad said performers are always working when everybody else is off. They would all try really hard to at least be together on Christmas. I remember Christmas was always a wonderful time, with a lot of presents and a whole lot of home-cooked food. My Aunt Mary and Aunt Sissy always made sure of that.

My dad's tight-knit family loved each other dearly, and you could see it every time they were together. Though they poked fun and razzed each other that they weren't playing their parts right, they truly had an unbreakable bond. I'm sure each and every one of them would credit my grandmother and grandfather for that love.

Dad's brothers and sisters carried this tradition on all through their lives. I have pictures of them jamming in my Aunt Mary's basement when they were all well into their seventies. At that point, most of us kids had become musicians ourselves, and got to sit in and experience those exceptional sessions.

Changing Times

J.L. Frank Passes Away

In May 1952 J.L. Frank and Pee Wee were on tour in Detroit when J.L. fell sick with a strep infection that restricted him to his hotel room. He told Pee Wee not to tell his wife Marie because he didn't want her to worry. During the night of May fourth, he had a massive heart attack and died in his hotel room at the age of 52.

Not only was he Pee Wee's manager and right arm, he was also his father-in-law and good friend. This was a devastating blow to Pee Wee, his wife and the Frank family. Suddenly Pee Wee found himself without a rudder to steer the ship. He was not used to playing the role of manager, and it became a daunting task to do both his role and J.L.'s, but he managed to get things under control.

Because J.L. died so young, his career was cut short, so not many today know the contributions he made to Country music. Despite this, the Country music industry did not forget him. A plaque of his induction into the Country Music Hall of Fame hangs close to Pee Wee King's.

J.L. Frank was one of the pioneers and an excellent promoter, manager and booking agent. He instituted a lot of skills that many repeated through the years. His techniques for drawing large crowds were phenomenal. He handled a lot of the bookings for the Grand Ole Opry, and if it looked like the hall wasn't going to be filled, he would send kids out into the streets to give away tickets to make sure the Opry was packed. He drew crowds in with attractions such as fiddling and yodeling contests.

In the beginning, the Opry charged no admission, but J.L. said not charging people admission devalued the show. If you require at least a small admission fee, the show becomes more valuable to the public. That's when the Opry took his advice and began charging admission.

J.L. pioneered in Country music and was worthy of his inclusion into the Country Music Hall of Fame.

In the music industry today it is quite normal for an artist to write, record and perform in several different bands. In the 1940s, this trend started to become popular. In 1949 my dad signed with King Records, a leading American independent record company and label founded in 1943 by Syd Nathan in Cincinnati, Ohio.

In the beginning, King Records specialized in Country music, at the time known as Hillbilly music. King advertised, "If it's a King, It's a Hillbilly—If it's a Hillbilly, it's a King."

This was my dad's first attempt to launch a solo career. Most musicians dream of having their own solo career, and my dad was probably no different. Knowing him the way I do, I would venture to say it was my mom's gentle nudge that convinced him to venture out. He played it smart and continued to perform with the Golden West Cowboys, which gave him a good stable foundation while he worked on his solo career.

For a short time he backed off from being the lead vocalist on the Golden West Cowboys recordings, but that didn't last long, and he was soon sharing the vocals along with his brother Gene.

Not long before he went solo he became a Kentucky Colonel, an honorary title given to an individual by approval of the governor of Kentucky. He named his band Redd Stewart and His Kentucky Colonels, mostly moonlighting Golden West Cowboy members.

When my brother was born in 1953, Mom and Dad named him Henry Redd Stewart, Jr., but everybody started calling him the Little Colonel. The name stuck so well that my parents actually had his name legally changed to Colonel Henry Redd Stewart, Jr. He has gone by Colonel from then until now with one exception—he is Uncle Corn to a special niece. I just refer to him as Cornball. But make no mistake, Cornball is well-loved in this family, as gentle and talented as my dad, a great musician in his own right.

Dad's first solo single released on King Records was "Blow Out All the Candles," which came out in the beginning of May. At the end of that month the songs "Alone" and "Perhaps It's Better That Way" were released. He continued to record solo for the King label, on which his singles were released on a regular basis until April 1951. Though none of these songs topped in the charts, they sold extremely well. He continued to play with the Golden West Cowboys through 1954 when he branched out again, this time recording solo for RCA Victor Records.

The 1950s brought an enormous amount of exposure for the Golden West Cowboys and a variety of projects. They did many recording sessions, ballroom appearances, television and radio shows, private parties, road shows and fairs. They performed on the *Kate Smith TV Show* from New York, and did a 26-week show from Cleveland, Ohio. They were all over the map!

In 1953 the Billboard Country & Western Disc Jockey Poll voted the Golden West Cowboys No. 1 favorite Country and Western band. Orchestra World also voted the Golden West Cowboys No. 1 Country and Western band of the year for 1949, 1950, 1951 and 1952.

In 1954 the Golden West Cowboys headlined the Barnyard Frolics from the 2,900-seat auditorium music hall in Little Rock, Arkansas to a standing room only crowd with at least a thousand more reportedly turned away. Those folks missed what *Billboard* called one of the hottest units in Western Swing that season.

In September 1955, Dad began his own half hour show on Chicago WBBM-TV every Thursday night. He received an offer from the producer to have his own show and decided he wanted to try it for a while. Dad not only led his own band, but did all of the arrangements, too. It added up to a lot of extra work, but he thoroughly enjoyed it. He brought in acts such as the Morgan

Sisters, the Wright Brothers and Randy Atcher. He still continued working with Pee Wee on various occasions, though.

As you can probably tell by now, my dad was one busy fellow. I remember Pee Wee telling me that during their years on the Grand Ole Opry, they were on the road 252 days of the year. Doing more television did lighten the load of traveling somewhat, but the TV shows made up for it because they took so much time and preparation.

In November 1954, I was born, so now my mom was home with three kids. You can only imagine the strain that Dad's constant activity put on our family. This is quite obvious from a letter my dad wrote to my mom. He told her she was right, it was time for him to consider the family, come off the road and try to find a normal job. Clearly, his traveling was putting a huge strain on their marriage.

So for a brief time he tried to make a living not playing music. He worked as a salesman for a car dealership, tried doing sales for a heating & air conditioning company, and also attempted to sell insurance. As my sister put it, he was not a salesman! Music was in his blood and what he was born to do. I've always said, stick with what you know, and that's what my dad knew best.

In 1957 he returned full-time as the lead vocalist for the Golden West Cowboys. Things were drastically changing in the music business and so was the music. The Golden West Cowboys, though still performing, were all but finished recording in the studios. Dad and Pee Wee returned to the studio to record, but this time without the band. Chet Atkins put together the musicians for the sessions and advised Pee Wee to forget those Golden West Cowboys.

In 1958 Pee Wee renamed the Golden West Cowboys. The group became Pee Wee King & His Band. The shows began to be billed featuring Redd Stewart. They added Minnie Pearl to the show and hit the road during a cross-country tour of fairs, auditoriums, parks, and festivals. They did state fairs all over the country, but most often performed at the Kentucky State Fair in Louisville.

The shows in Louisville featured Tom T. Hall, Crystal Gayle, and many other top talents in a show sponsored by Phillip Morris. They also performed regularly at the William H. King Sport, Boat & Vacation Show in Louisville for many years. So much for selling cars! In 1959 Dad tried his hand again at a new solo album titled *Redd Stewart Sings Old-Time Favorite Tunes* for the Audio Lab Record Label.

It is amazing how many miles this duo traveled, how much music they wrote and how much they achieved in their 20 years together from the 1930s to the 1950s. One has to remember they did all of this before YouTube, the Internet, cable TV, computers, high-tech recording software and mass marketing.

Most of their travels occurred on the back roads in old beat up cars and trucks with no air conditioning or any of the modern conveniences we have today. Neither Pee Wee nor my dad in their later years considered themselves 'stars' or anything special. They would both tell you, "We were just trying to make a living."

Instead they made history, and they didn't even know it.

When we were growing up, we had absolutely no clue who my dad really was. He was a master at keeping his professional life separate from his private life. When he was in town and spent time with us, it was all about us kids. There was never any mention of what he did on the road.

If we asked him any questions about what he did, his answers were very brief and revealed very little. He would always turn the conversation back to us. He wanted to know what was going on in our lives and wanted to be a part of it. If you had asked me when I was young if my dad was a star, I would have laughed and responded, "No way!"

To me he was just a musician who played in a band for a living. To us, our dad was simply Dad. But one day my sister had a real eye-opening experience as to our father's public identity. Lydia wrote this story about that particular day.

"I was a teenager in the 1960s, and I was accompanying my father to a show at the old Armory in Louisville. I believe it was called the Phillip Morris Festival and it was held a few weeks before the Kentucky Derby. I was so excited! Not only was I wearing new shoes with a heel of at least two inches, but I was allowed to wear lipstick again. That was something I was only permitted to do on special occasions. And let me tell you, this was a *very* special event. I was going to see Jerry Lee Lewis!!

Oh sure, daddy was going to play too, but that really didn't impress me. I knew he was a musician and traveled a lot. He was with Pee Wee King's band and Pee Wee played the accordion. My daddy played fiddle or guitar, whichever was needed for the particular show they were doing. It was Country music.

Jerry Lee Lewis played Rock n Roll! That's where I was—rocking and rolling. Who really cared about Country music? It was kind of corny. I mean, everyone knew Elvis was the king. Just because Uncle Pee Wee's last name was King didn't make it so.

We walked into the rear doors where all the musicians entered. There was a flurry of people moving about, pushing carts loaded with amplifiers, musical instruments, and microphones. There were people everywhere and all of them seemed to have a mission—a chore to do or a place to go. I had to be very careful not to slip as the floor was concrete which was very smooth either from the wear of activity over the years or because it was constructed that way. My new shoes with the heels were somewhat slippery, and I really wasn't used to walking in them.

I was having a difficult time taking in everything as people were moving so fast and they were much taller than I was. The sounds were amazing. There were musicians tuning their instruments, setting up their amplifiers, and just generally talking with other performers and workers. Through all of the people and commotion I kept my eyes peeled for "him." I knew "he" would be among all these people and I could hardly wait to be able to see him in person.

Suddenly there were women screaming and yelling. Oh my heavens it must be him—it must be Jerry Lee Lewis. As I moved closer to my daddy, I looked to my right in the direction of the screams. All I could see was dozens of women running in our direction—screaming and yelling at the same time. Quickly I looked to my left—fully expecting to see Mr. Lewis himself. But there was no one there. *No one!* I looked back to my right and all those screaming women were within feet of daddy and me.

Unbelievable! They were rushing to my father! Not Jerry Lee Lewis—but to *my father!* He was signing autographs, having his picture taken with them, and chatting casually as they oohed and awed all over him. He was smiling at me, too. I suppose he saw the astonished look on my face and realized what was going on in my head.

As I stood there watching my daddy, I saw my father in a different way. Suddenly I realized he was a star, and that he had fans who adored him, and he was more than just my daddy. I was so proud. Somehow he looked different at that moment than I had ever seen him. He was so handsome. And he *was* a star!

I did get to see Jerry Lee Lewis that day and even had my picture taken with him. He was very tall and had almost white-blonde hair. He did have women screaming after him. And he did have a colorful wardrobe too, but somehow, the thrill of meeting the "*him*" was overshadowed by me seeing the real star—my father."

Howard Johnson's Disaster

I think it is safe to say that all of us have done something in public to embarrass our parents, but when one of your parents just happens to be a Country music star, the word embarrassing takes on a whole new meaning.

This scene takes place in the early 1960s in Louisville, Kentucky when my father was home from touring on the road. After 10 years on the Opry, a bunch of hits like *Tennessee Waltz* and "You Belong to Me," and almost 30 years of performing, he had become very well known, especially in Louisville. Out in public, it was commonplace for people to come up and ask for Dad's autograph.

When my dad was in town, the very first thing he wanted to do was take his family out to dinner. The Howard Johnson's Restaurant, his favorite place, was classy in those days. Since we went there a lot, everyone knew who he was.

Now, picture my dad sitting there with his wife and three kids in a busy restaurant trying to enjoy a well-deserved dinner, when suddenly my brother comes up with a brainstorm idea. So he asks for permission to go to the bathroom, grabs his partner in crime (that would be me), and off we go to destroy my dad's evening.

When we get to the bathroom my brother unveils his diabolical plan. Being young and dumb, I agree this would be a very cool thing to do. Here is the plan: take all of the toilet paper rolls we could find, clog up the toilets and sinks, and then flush the toilets and turn on all of the faucets so the sinks would run over.

We also decided it would be a great idea to lock all of the bathroom stall doors and crawl out from underneath. Great plan, right?

86

After completing our task, we headed back to the table to join the family as if nothing were wrong.

As you can imagine, we were snickering, which tipped off Mom that something was up. She asked, "What did you two boys do in that bathroom?" Our faces got straight as a ruler and she knew something was amiss. At this point, we all noticed quite a commotion going on by the bathroom door as the restaurant employees frantically tried to stop the river of water flowing from the men's bathroom.

Dad looked at Mom, Mom looked at Dad, and they both glared at us with an expression that could kill you right there on the spot. With so much commotion, they used the opportunity to head for the door and whisk us off to the house.

Now, I must tell you that my father was one of the most gentle people I have ever met. Getting angry was just not in his DNA. But this night was an exception!

My brother and I were removed from under our beds, which we hid under as soon as we got inside, and our butts got up-close and personal with Dad's rhinestone-covered cowboy belt. I don't remember if my father ever confessed to the management that his sons were the ones who flooded their restaurant, but I don't remember eating there anymore, either.

A Different Kind of Life

The story I just told you about the Howard Johnson's fiasco was very funny, for sure, and I am pretty sure that's not the only thing we did to embarrass my dad in public. Sometimes I feel like that fiasco may have been the straw that broke the camel's back, because there was big trouble brewing between my mom and dad.

It's no secret to anyone that the music business is extremely tough on marriages. As I grew up, my dad seemed more like an uncle that came to stay with us on occasion. Don't get me wrong, I knew he was my dad, but when I look back, that's what it felt like. He was on the road more than three-fourths of the year, and when he was in town there were public appearances, TV shows and studio time.

This left very little time for family life and an enormous amount of strain on my mom, who had to hold down the fort while he was away. It also made for a very lonely life for the one left at home, the same reason why so many military couples end up in divorce.

In 1962 when I was eight years old, my parents called it quits. Not much really changed for me, but for my mother it was a different story. She loved my dad more than life, but it just wasn't working anymore. To my parents' credit, they did an amazing job of keeping the family together.

Though they no longer lived together, they continued to work as a team to ensure that us kids were well taken care of and loved. They both played a role in raising us and provided great role models. If there was any fighting between them, it was kept from us, and things seemed to be normal, pretty much the way they had always been.

For the first several years, Dad was always there to share Christmas with us and spent time with us every time he was in town. He helped my mom buy a new house on the east side of town, and even closed in a screened porch to make an extra bedroom. Little did I know at that time that my future wife Sharon lived only a few blocks away!

The older my father got, the more conservative he became and the stronger he grew in his faith. My mother, on the other hand, was strong in her faith but far more liberal than Dad. Looking back now, I can see that it wasn't simply life on the road that destroyed their marriage. They had become two different people. But life goes on and so did ours.

My dad and Pee Wee continued performing at fairs, entertainment halls, boat shows, community events and TV shows. At this stage of the game Pee Wee had been performing for close to 30 years, and my dad was right behind him, so they were starting to wind down. So far I've only talked about their biggest hits, but their song catalogs are much bigger than that. My dad's catalog alone has close to 400 songs. Many of these became big hits for the band.

They had achieved more than they ever could have imagined. Dad's studio walls held numerous awards for his achievements in the music business. Who would ever have thought a young teenager from Wisconsin could team up with a southern boy from Tennessee and achieve so much? And Dad accomplished all of this with only a seventh grade education.

My father had a lifetime songwriting contract with Acuff/Rose Publishing, Inc. One way that songwriters earned extra income back then was to write music for a publisher as staff writers. They received a flat fee for writing songs that the publisher would then give to performers who didn't write their own music. The original songwriter could claim no copyrights because they had been paid up front to write the music.

After my dad died in 2003, I had the pleasure of speaking by phone with Roy Ayres. Two things he said always stick in my memory. First, "Your dad was the gold in the Golden West Cowboys." Secondly, "Your dad actually wrote well over 1,000 songs." He said that some of the hits back in those days were actually written by my dad, but as a staff writer, he was unable to claim them.

I have had several people over the years tell me that they swore

Dad wrote one of the biggest hits back then. I will not name the song or the artist who recorded it, because I don't know this to be a fact. But a songwriter, especially my dad, usually has a very unique writing style.

His style is recognizable almost immediately. In his later years he recorded this big hit I've mentioned. I went back and listened to his version, and could not wipe the smile off my face. If my dad had been in the room I would have turned to him and grinned, "You wrote that song, didn't you?"

As we grew into adults, things continued on pretty much the way they always had. The only difference was that when Dad came into town, we would visit him. He would go out of his way to make those times as special as possible.

I found out he was a really good cook. He had a spaghetti sauce to die for. It would take him about six hours to prepare, but it was well worth the time and effort. Everybody also raved about his recipe for Roquefort dressing, but my favorite recipe was his steak sauce, and he taught me how to make it.

It is extremely simple, but oh so good! The funny thing about this recipe is that you have to mix it to taste. I couldn't tell you the measurements for the simple three ingredients, but only know how it's supposed to taste. The three ingredients are ketchup, Heinz 57 sauce and sugar. Like I said, extremely simple, but you have to know how it's supposed to taste in order to make it.

In 1962 before we moved from the house where I was born, we had a very special Christmas. I was eight years old when our parents divorced, and the last Christmas was one I will always remember. My dad made sure he was in town, and my parents went overboard with gifts.

I remember that the doorway to the hall in our house on Norbourne had an actual door, which you don't see too often today. My brother Colonel and I were still masters at mischief. Now, I must state here that my brother always led our antics, and I was just too dumb to say no.

On some past Christmases, we would get up before my parents and sneak out into the living room to peak at the gifts. We would shake the boxes, try to guess what was in them, and became proficient at opening the ends to peek in and find out what the gift was.

Then we would close them back up so no one would ever know, or so we thought. It didn't take long for my parents to catch on to what we were doing, so they put a little latch at the top of the door so we couldn't open it.

Colonel and I were determined to beat that latch, so we would quietly drag out little pieces of furniture and stack them up so we could reach the latch. Unfortunately, that plan never did work. We just couldn't get the pile high enough before my parents heard all the commotion and stopped us.

On this special Christmas, we had no choice but to wait until they got up. Two things made this Christmas so special. Colonel wanted a set of drums and I wanted a guitar, so the anticipation was driving us nuts. When the door finally flew open, we both rushed into the living room towards the Christmas tree with our gifts.

Somehow my parents must have gotten confused, because the drums were on my side and the guitar on Colonel's. I think Colonel and I must have had a memory lapse, because I jumped on those drums as though they were just what I was waiting for. Colonel did the same with the guitar, but my dad quickly stepped in and said, "Wait boys, I think we got these backwards."

But we both agreed this was exactly what we wanted. This was the beginning of my musical journey, and my brother's as well. I have to laugh because most parents would have bought "toy" instruments to start their kids on, but not our dad. Oh no, he wasn't having any part of that!

My drum set, a fully decked out, beautiful blue Ludwig set, had all the whistles and bells. Colonel's guitar was a 1962 Gibson SG special, which guitar players today would pay big bucks to have. It had a beautiful transparent red stained mahogany body, something to behold.

Though the instruments starred in this show, the room was packed with gifts. We even got our own Green Beret outfits complete with rifles. My parents truly made that Christmas a special time. The divorce had been hard on all of us, and this was their way to try and make up for it.

That holiday will always hold a special place in my heart because it was one of the best Christmases I remember, but it was also the start of the musical journey I am still on today.

As a result of the divorce, we began to learn things about our dad that we never knew. When my parents were married, he was working a lot more than in the 1960s, so his trips home were all about us kids. He spent the time taking us places, going to restaurants, and generally having a good time. Doing the things he wanted to do was always put on the back burner.

Things became completely different when we visited him now. First, he wasn't working quite as much, so he had a little more time. We got to see hobbies that we had never seen, he would cook for us, which was very unusual, and shared a little more of his life and what he was doing. We started seeing Dad in a whole new light, and that was a good thing.

One of the first discoveries I remember really stunned me. I was out with him by myself and he needed to run by his apartment, which I had never seen. When we got there, he showed me around. When we walked into his bedroom, the first thing I noticed was a pistol on his dresser. I had never seen him with a gun before and didn't know he knew anything about guns.

At this stage, no one had ever told me that he served in the military. He wasn't a hunter, so this was rather shocking. When I asked him about the pistol, he simply said, "This is not the safest neighborhood around, so I have it for protection." I had always considered my dad to be a very gentle, peaceful man. Seeing his gun altered my perception in a good way. From that point on he looked a little more like a cowboy to me. Those cowboy outfits he wore were starting to make more sense.

My sister Lydia had similar memories of learning new things

about Dad after the divorce. Here is an example in her own words.

"It's funny what things pop into my mind when I try to think of some of Daddy's favorite things, like what foods he liked. The first thing I can remember is when I went to see him for the first overnight visit after my parents were divorced. It was a little apartment that he had just rented in south Louisville, and I remember it being very plain and simply furnished.

There was no carpet on the floor, just hardwood floors that were waxed and shining even though there were worn areas from many years of use. The floor squeaked when you walked across some of the boards. It was the first time I had ever seen an apartment from the inside, and I remember thinking it was okay for my Daddy to live in. He would be comfortable there. He would be safe there. He wasn't in town very often so this would be okay.

He had lived a little while in a tiny trailer before he found this apartment. He took me there once, and I hated the idea of him living there. It was so tiny and old, and the place it was parked at was not a good feeling place. I remember thinking why did he have to live like this? Surely, he didn't live there because he liked it. It was awful! It was so small I couldn't stay the night as it only had one bed. It just wasn't a place for my Daddy to be. He never liked a lot of frills and never valued expensive things just because they had a brand name or had big price tags. He did value quality and things of beauty. And for him, simple was just perfect.

After the grand tour of the apartment, we got in the car and drove out to a place where you could buy fresh fish. He picked out what seemed to be a special piece of haddock, and they carefully wrapped it with as much care as he used in selecting it. We went back to the apartment and he began to prepare dinner. He never cooked at home before, so I was somewhat hesitant as I watched the preparations begin. I remember how carefully he rubbed the fish with oil, and then put thin slices of lemon on top. A little salt and pepper, and then into the oven it went. I remember how he talked about what the oil did to seal the juices in the fish, and how important the lemon was to give it a special taste. I can't remember a single other thing we had with that wonderful piece of fish, but I suppose it really doesn't matter. That piece of fish carries more memories than any side dish could.

I'm sure we had some bread with our meal. Daddy *always* had bread with every meal. And of course, we had dessert, but we didn't eat it until later that night. It was one of his favorite 'treats.' It was great fun to assemble this delicacy, peanut butter and Hershey bar sandwich. You had to use specific things to make it just perfect—creamy peanut butter, certainly not chunky, the real Hershey chocolate bar, plain no almonds, and of course really fresh soft white bread. You had to put a thin layer of peanut butter on both pieces of bread, and then the chocolate in between the two pieces of bread. Oh, so good! Oh, so rich! But it was 'our' special treat. As I said before, my dad loved simple things of beauty, and believe me, that piece of fish and 'our' special treat fit the description of beauty.

We never talked much about why Mom and Dad separated and ultimately divorced after so many years of marriage. I was 16 years old at the time, but it was an era when children didn't know their parents' business, like how much money they made or what they had to pay for their cars and houses. I was never allowed to know how much my daddy made when he worked. I remember him asking me if I had ever seen a $100 bill before, and of course I had to say, 'Heavens no!' That was like a million dollar bill now. I remember thinking we must be very rich for daddy to have one of those bills. But I do remember him saying he wouldn't have it long because he had to pay some bills. I never knew what bills, or how much they were, we just weren't allowed to know. It was considered adult business.

I know we lived in a nice house in a nice neighborhood. We had a TV and a fenced in yard for our dog, and we had a canary in a cage that hung in the kitchen by the windows. We had a new car most of the time, once we even had a Cadillac. It was green and had some pretty big fins on it! I remember Mom telling me later when I got older that in 1953 Daddy had walked into the showroom and paid cash—$700!!"

A Career Highlight

Redd and Pee Wee · The woman who was the inspiration behind the song

"The Tennessee Waltz" becomes the state song of Tennessee

In the early 1960s, my dad and Pee Wee continued performing as always, but there was something big stirring. They were in Columbia, SC when they received a phone call from Wesley Rose, their publisher.

He said, "Boys, I think you'd better get back home because something incredible is about to happen. Make sure you're in Nashville by tomorrow morning. The Governor has proposed the *Tennessee Waltz* as the state song, and the legislature is about to vote. Everyone here believes it will pass."

Early the next morning they headed to the airport and asked if there was any way they could get a flight to Nashville. They learned that a gentleman was servicing a private plane to head that way. So, they hitched a ride and made it to Nashville. Acuff/Rose Publishing Company had a taxi waiting to take them to the state capitol.

On February 17, 1965, the Tennessee legislature made the *Tennessee Waltz* the official state song. What an incredible moment for my dad and Pee Wee, and a high point in their career. It was especially meaningful to my dad because he was born in Tennessee. Until 1965, Tennessee had only adapted three state songs, but they were all recognized only regionally.

This changed when they adapted the *Tennessee Waltz*, a national bestselling song that the whole nation recognized. A perfect fit for the state of Tennessee.

For a songwriter, this is a once-in-a-lifetime event. Very few have one of their songs chosen as a state song. Whenever I think about this, I picture that little country boy in his straw hat with a fiddle in his gunnysack walking down that alley to the radio station and the life-changing event bumping into J.L. Frank. Look how far that little boy has come!

Becoming successful and being really good at your craft sometimes comes with some bad side effects. One of those is getting
too big for your britches. Such was the case in 1963 when Pee Wee,
at the advice of some friends, decided to try his hand at making a
movie. Big mistake!

Pee Wee pitched the idea for his Country Western Hoedown
movie to his manager, Bill King and his lawyer, Chris Duvall. It
was real simple story set in a western hotel where people came from
all over the U.S. to stay and be entertained by Country music stars.
Bill King was against the idea from the start. He basically told Pee
Wee this was the last thing he needed to do.

So Pee Wee talked to Chris Duvall, and the more they talked,
the more he got excited about the movie. Together they convinced
Bill King to go along with the idea.

Pee Wee brought in a director and musicians, singers and actors
from all over the country. All the indoor scenes were shot in a studio
in Louisville, Kentucky and all the outdoor scenes at Renfro Valley.

Pee Wee's first mistake was counting on his friends to let him use
their songs, but it wasn't until the movie was done that he found
out they couldn't legally give him the rights. Only the publishers
could do that. As soon as the movie was completed, he got hit with
a slew of lawsuits.

The money started adding up, and Pee Wee was going to have
to pay staggering permissions and penalties. The actual making of
the film had been exciting. The low point came when he learned
what he was going to have to pay to settle with everybody.

All of this took a while, so they were finally able to release the movie in 1967, but by then the film was dead. They did everything they knew to promote it, but couldn't even give it away. This venture turned into a complete disaster.

They tried to advertise in some of the trade publications, calling the movie The Happiest Wildest Country-Western Rip-Snorting Shingdig to come your way with 33 hit songs and 15 top stars from the stages of 7 National Barn Dances. They included the Golden West Cowboys, the Collins Sisters, Bonnie Sloan, Ginger Callahan, Jack Leonard, Red Murphy, Eller Long, Redd Stewart and many others.

William R. Johnson directed the movie, and it was filmed in Eastman Color. However, the promoters had no clue what they were doing, so Pee Wee ended up having to promote and distribute it himself.

He didn't make a dime. As a matter of fact, he took a huge beating. He also produced a souvenir album to sell at the theaters where the film was playing, and it did better than the movie. When all attempts had failed to turn a profit, he took it to his old friend, Gene Autry.

Gene laughed and said, "Pee Wee, with all of your experience, you should have known better." That was the last time Pee Wee ever attempted to make a movie. I think he learned that if you're going to do something, make sure you use professionals who know what they're doing. Lesson learned.

In 1968 my dad signed with Hickory Records. This felt like coming home to him, because the parent company was Acuff/Rose Publishing. He always loved Acuff/Rose because they really cared about their writers and took good care of them. They were not real strict like most publishing companies, which gave him the ability to be creative. They were also extremely honest. So, signing with Hickory Records was a perfect fit.

While he continued to perform with Pee Wee, he began writing his own material for a solo album to release in the future. The music industry, especially Country music, was changing rapidly, and I can tell by the music Dad wrote that he was fighting to adapt. His wardrobe changed, his writing changed, and he even changed his hairstyle.

I've followed music all my life, and have seen this happen over and over and over again. Change is inevitable and once an artist has established himself and had good success, changing with the times does not come easily. Only a handful are successful at this.

The recording sessions my dad did now were far more elaborate than those he had done with Pee Wee. Technology had changed quite a bit, so the recordings were way more polished. The use of many more instruments, background singers, and new production techniques gave him a much bigger sound than anything he had created in the past. His voice had deepened some from the earlier years, which gave it a warmer, smoother, more soothing sound. One person described his tone as smooth as honey. His voice was in tiptop shape, and this showed in every one of his recordings.

My dad put his heart and soul into these new recordings. Pee

Wee was beginning to slow down, as he was nine years older. I'm sure Dad was concerned about how long the Redd Stewart and Pee Wee King team would last, so he developed a plan to go solo. The question was, would the alterations he made in sound enough to make the difference? Only time would tell.

The End of the Golden West Cowboys

In 1969 after years of being the bandleader, Pee Wee decided to put the Golden West Cowboys to rest. My dad and Pee Wee continued performing but hired musicians as their backup band. Their songwriting success afforded them the ability to slow down. Those wonderful things called royalties gave them the necessary financial support. No longer did they have to travel hundreds of miles, hundreds of days a year to pay the bills. Success was sweet!

Pee Wee began to spend more time working on the business side of the music industry, while my dad dug into songwriting. This newfound freedom gave more time for hobbies, golfing and collaborating with other musicians and songwriters.

By this time, Dad had become a self-taught master musician. His knowledge of music theory was mind blowing. His skills on the instruments he played were second to none. He could play guitar with the best of them, including players like Chet Atkins and Roy Clark. I was told that sidemen in other bands were extremely intimidated by him.

They would all be backstage tuning their instruments, waiting to perform, and my dad would walk in, pick up his guitar, grab his polishing rag and slowly polish the neck of his guitar while they all watched. He would tune up and start warming up his fingers. Watching him play a guitar was something to behold. His fingers would dance across the strings like a ballerina on a stage, and his technical skills were quite amazing. He was a hard act to follow.

It was around this time that he began to stick his toe into the water of teaching guitar lessons. If I remember correctly, his first student lived next door, and his name was Dallas. I remember going

107

to Dad's house, hearing Dallas play, and being amazed at what my dad had taught him. I think this first student sparked an idea that later would become a passion. Dad loved to help people, and this was a way to do it.

A good example of his teaching passion came to me years later at an event in Nashville, representing my dad for *Tennessee Waltz*. I was seated next to Jett Williams, Hank Williams Sr.'s daughter. I knew who she was from pictures, and that Dad and Hank were friends. They had both recorded each other's songs through the years.

So, I leaned over and told her that my dad knew her dad. She asked, "Who was your dad?" When I told her Redd Stewart, you would have thought she just won the lottery. Her face lit up like a spotlight. She grabbed my knee and said, "Oh my God, you don't know how much your daddy has helped me through the years!"

She said when she was starting out, she performed at some of the same shows as my dad and he spent time with her backstage teaching her guitar techniques. She said he was always encouraging, telling her not to be nervous. She even got a chance to go to his home in Louisville, and they corresponded back and forth quite often.

I've met other musicians with similar stories about how Dad helped them when they were starting out. Like I said, he loved to help people, and never hesitated to share his knowledge.

Humbled & Grateful

Redd Stewart receiving
Nashville Songwriters Award
in 1970.

Looking back over my dad's career always intrigues me. If you split it into decades, there seems to be a big event in each one that affected his career and life. In the '60s, *Tennessee Waltz* became the state song. The '50s were when Patti Page recorded *Tennessee Waltz*, catapulting it to one of the biggest Country music hits ever written.

In that same decade, Dad and Pee Wee wrote their other biggest hits—"Slow Poke," "Bonaparte's Retreat," and "You Belong to Me." In the '40s, Dad met my mom, and as a result wrote the immortal *Tennessee Waltz*. The '30s contained that chance meeting in the alleyway with J.L. Frank that brought Dad and Pee Wee together.

The '70s were no different. The beginning of this decade started off with a bang. The Nashville Songwriters Hall of Fame was born in this year, an enterprise of the fledging Nashville Songwriters Association. A credentials committee selected a charter class of 21 writers to be inducted on Monday, October 12, 1970 at the first Hall of Fame Banquet and Ceremony at the Holiday Inn–Vanderbilt. There were about 50 guests, and the emcee was radio personality Biff Collie.

Among those 21 artists at this prestigious event were my dad and Pee Wee King. Some others were Hank Williams, Bob Wills, Ernest Tubb, Jimmie Rodgers, Fred Rose and Gene Autry. My dad was honored to be inducted into the Hall of Fame along with such big names in the music business.

Over the years, the Nashville Songwriters Hall of Fame grew to be one of the most sought-after honors a songwriter in the Nashville music community could desire. The Hall of Fame's purpose is to educate, celebrate, and archive the achievements and contributions made by the members of the Nashville Songwriters Hall of Fame.

We have a picture of my dad receiving his plaque at the ceremony, and the smile on his face says it all. This was truly a huge event in his career. He had come a long way from that little boy in the straw hat!

The year 1971 proved to be another eventful year in Dad's life. Many years before, he performed with a singing and dancing act of two sisters known as the Collins Sisters. Minnie Pearl was with Pee Wee at the time and thought the sisters would be a great addition to the show. Pee Wee hired them and they remained with the show until my dad and Pee Wee retired.

In '71, Darlene Collins became Dad's wife. Not long after they married, they built a house on the east side of Louisville and Dad built his first real home studio in the basement. Every time I went to visit, I was impressed at the crafting talent of Darlene and her sister Joyce. Joyce lived with them for many years, making it easier when they performed on the road. Rehearsing for upcoming shows was much easier because they were all in the same place.

When they weren't on the road, Darlene and Joyce spent some of their time making things, like custom-made appliance covers for the kitchen and gorgeous flower arrangements. But one of their most unique creations were custom red amp covers with Dad's name hand-sewn in each for all of his amplifiers. Very classy!

They were always gracious hosts, made us feel at home, and served delicious homemade meals. Darlene gave Dad one of his most treasured gifts, a beautiful white Baby Grand piano that sat in their living room. The first time I ever saw him play that piano, he played an intricate classical piece. I was shocked that he had taught himself such a complicated composition. It was incredible to watch his mastery.

I Remember

Being a songwriter myself, I know full well the anticipation after months of writing, recording and editing songs that have become your babies. A lot of hard work goes into creating music for other people's enjoyment. I'm astonished that in today's world, some people out there believe they should be able to listen to your music for free.

If they only knew the years of training in both instrument playing and songwriting, and what it takes just to reach the point where you can record. The money spent on equipment, studio musicians, producers and mastering technicians is enormous, and the competition fierce.

In 1972, after four years of writing and recording in between shows, my dad finally completed what I consider one of his best solo releases. This album testifies to his musical and songwriting skills and his unique voice. For the first time, he was able to do a full-production solo album with all the available new technology. The end result was an awesome album.

I know full well the work he put into this recording, and his high hopes for its success. At the same time, the fear of complete rejection or a mediocre response can instantly kill one's confidence, especially with so much sweat equity to bring songs to life.

He titled this album *I Remember*, the title cut. Though it had great reviews, it did not come close to performing as he anticipated. When I look back now at where music was in the '70s, people just weren't buying that brand of Country music anymore.

I don't think Hickory Records put forth the marketing efforts this album needed or it could have been much more successful. I say this album was Country music, but it was actually a cross between Country and Pop. Some songs depict more of a Frank Sinatra or Dean Martin style.

Fans of my dad and Pee Wee were not used to this mix. I fully believe this was Dad's attempt to catch up with the times and be relevant with the music of the day, but sadly, his efforts fell short. I believe that anyone listening to this album would say, "Why in the world did it not go gold?"

After my dad passed away in 2003, I took the original *I Remember* album, one of the good old vinyl records of the '70s, and digitalized it to put into my computer. I had a small project studio in my home, and using my limited skills, re-mastered each song to make the recordings sound more up-to-date.

My wife and I then created a 12-page full color booklet and hired a graphic artist to design the artwork for the CD pressing company. Once we got the finished CDs, we distributed them to disc jockeys in hopes of getting more airplay. We made a limited amount available for online purchase, and also sent some CDs to people who reviewed new releases.

Consider this sampling of reviews this CD received:

"This collection proves what a talent Redd Stewart was."
~Reviewed in the United States on August 31, 2005 by K. Loftis

"Redd Stewart wrote songs straight from his heart, with beauty, thoughtfulness, often humor, and always unflinching integrity. That fact is made evident on this lovingly compiled CD, which contains a treasury of some of Redd's favorite compositions, and many of his most beloved works.

Redd was not only a fantastic writer, but also a wonderful singer. I liken his voice to warm molasses dripping from hot biscuits. His voice rings with soulful sincerity, tenderness and wit. All of these qualities can be found in the title track "I Remember," a lovely little song that is sure to bring a smile to the lips of any listener. As on all the songs featured here, Redd's gift for crafting a superb melody is evident on this song.

The second track, "Bimbo," is an absolute delight. You're sure to be left singing the chorus for hours after the song ends. Whoever could resist this little gem of a song?

"Having Second Thoughts" has a highly singable melody, and as always, Redd's vocal is top-notch. A song of lost love, it is sure to impress.

"Sunshine Over the Hill" is a wonderfully optimistic song, with a bit of a soul element thrown in for good measure. The following track, "My Home Is the Dust of The Road," soars with a glorious string arrangement underlying Redd's superb vocal.

What can I possibly say about *Tennessee Waltz* that hasn't been said time and time again? It's a simply superb song that may leave a tear in your eye. Again, the absolute integrity in Redd's delivery of this song makes it so fantastic.

"Banjo" is a wonderful story song sure to draw in the listener. "Dreaming Again" is a love song that you'll be singing all day, while "Cold, Cold Heart" exhibits a longing quality that makes it timeless.

"Talk to The Angels" is so tender and vulnerable that it will break your heart, and the closing track, the delightful "Bonaparte's Retreat" may have you dancing like the song's characters!

Redd's timelessness as a songwriter and the absolute beauty of both his songs and his voice are showcased beautifully in this sterling recording. I for one look forward to many more albums like this to commemorate Redd's music. This lovingly compiled CD is proof positive that the man and his music are truly unforgettable."

I've listened to the *I Remember* album many times, and every time I sit back and say, "This was my dad at his best!" This album holds a special place in my heart because it was one of his best works, and I got the chance to make it just a little bit better when I re-mastered it into a CD.

Many years ago, I was contacted by a DJ for an interview. We had sent him one of the CDs, and he must have been impressed enough to contact me. Before the interview began, he complimented the incredible work my dad had done on this album.

He asked where it had been recorded because it sounded as though it was recorded in this day and age. He said, 'I don't remember recordings in the '70s sounding like this.' I proceeded to tell him that I had re-mastered it. He then told me that his engineer was extremely impressed by the quality of the recording.

When the interview was over, I had a really good laugh, because to be honest with you, I didn't have a clue what I was doing. I used the little bit of knowledge I had and trusted my ears to guide me to the sound I was looking for. I guess I hit the mark. I hope Dad was proud.

Sixteen years later, my recording skills and studio are ten times what they were back then. Maybe I should take a shot at it again!

Simple Man, Simple Studio

My dad was not really suited for fame, not your typical Country & Western star. He was a normal guy, kind of like your neighborhood insurance agent or plumber. He was about as simple a person as you could imagine, the most gentle-spirited man I think I ever met. He never had a cross word for anybody, and it took a whole heck of a lot to get him angry, and even then it was not what you would expect.

I think a lot of this came from his life during the Depression. He went through some hard times growing up, and knew what it was like to be hungry and in need. He had to fight every inch of the way up the ladder to success. For him to have his first band at fourteen years old is a testament to what he had to do to make it. He was extremely grateful for everything he had and for everything he achieved.

My dad was a man of faith, and not about to waste any of God's money given to him. This was extremely evident in his home studio. Now, here is a guy who at the time could have afforded the biggest and best of instruments and equipment, but that was not the case.

First off, I can never remember Dad owning more than three electric guitars at one time. His main guitar was an Epiphone Sheraton, definitely not the top of the line. For as long as I can remember, that was the guitar he played. In earlier pictures of him performing, I have seen him with a few other guitars, but they were very short lived.

That Epiphone now sits in the Nashville Country Music Hall of Fame. When we donated it, I got to hold it one last time and it was touching how old and worn it was—so old there were spider web cracks throughout the finish. The Whammy bar had broken off years before and never replaced. Why he never bought a new one is beyond me.

There was one time he spent a little extra money and got himself a Gibson 335, all you musicians out there know the guitar I'm talking about, but Dad barely played it. I think he used that guitar more as a backup in case the Epiphone went down. He tried his hand at a solid-body electric made by Peavey, a T-60, but complained it was way too heavy to hold, so it, too, sat on the sidelines.

In his home studio he had one bass guitar, two electrics, one acoustic, Old Joe Clark's banjo, and that was it. He kept his prized Baby Grand Piano up in the living room. In my studio today, to the left of my desk, sits an early 1960s Fender Super Reverb amplifier that belonged to Dad. This was his amplifier for years and years and years. The amps built in the '60s weighed a ton, and it always intrigued me that such a little guy, at 5'3", could cart that amp around from show to show, but Dad did. The only reason he stopped using it was because he got too old to carry it, so he kept it in his studio and bought one of the new Peavey lightweight amps.

He had a very small Casio keyboard that looked more like a toy compared to the keyboards I use today. He had one of the simplest drum machines you've ever seen, more like a glorified metronome. He also had a reverb unit from Radio Shack, of all places!

For recording, he had two four-track reel-to-reel tape recorders and a few sets of speakers that really belonged on a home stereo system, nothing like the studio monitors you find today. There also were a couple of microphone stands and inexpensive microphones, plus a few other odds and ends, but that was about it.

The one thing I took away from all this was that the guy was so good he didn't need any fancy equipment to write the music that came from his head. His studio was simply for laying down ideas. He would let the pros at the studios handle the technical side of things. He concentrated on the music more than the production, and when I think about it, many of us today probably get too caught up in production and don't pay enough attention to the music.

In that simple little studio, he recorded some amazing songs, some of which have never been released. I hope to change that in the near future. When I was in my teens, my brother and I began to write songs, and when we would go to visit, Dad would record us. It always thrilled us that he made us sound so good on such a simple system.

A few years after I got married, I revealed to my dad that I wanted to pursue music as a career. He sat back and gave me that look he always gave me when he disapproved. He said, "Son, promise me right here and now that you will never do music for a career. You keep a real job and take care of your family because you don't want anything to do with this business. It's a long hard road to the top, and it's even harder to stay there once you get there."

Not five minutes later, he turned around with that spark in his eye and said, "But then again, it only takes one hit!" What in the world was I supposed to take away from that? The conversation drifted to something else and I never got a chance to ask him what he meant.

I did, however, take his advice and never made music for a living. The desire was there because I was just like him, but I knew in my heart he was right.

Another humorous example of Dad's thriftiness was a closet in his studio. Inside he kept just about every box for every item he ever bought for his home studio and office, complete with instructions and the warranty card. I used to think to myself, "This is a fire hazard, what is my dad thinking?" I guess he figured that if anything went wrong with a piece of gear, instead of buying a new one, he was going to send it back for repair.

After Dad passed away, my brother, my sister and I traveled back to Louisville to go through his things. When we walked into the studio, the first thing I noticed was that everything looked as if he had just stepped away for a moment and was coming right back to continue his work. Some instruments were out, a microphone still in its stand, and a paper on the desk with some lyrics scribbled on it, with a pencil nearby.

It had been a few years since Dad had ever been down there. He had taken a fall down the steps to that studio that eventually made him bedridden. It was heart wrenching to know that Darlene loved him so much that she completely expected him to get well, and she would see him back in that studio creating new music again. She left everything just the way it was.

Two Fellows Mopping the Stage

I just told you how simple and normal my dad really was, but I must give credit where credit is due. Pee Wee was just like him. I think these two were so much alike that their long-term relationship was destiny. Neither one ever considered themselves big stars. The following story proves just that.

They were performing at a fairgrounds or some type of outdoor venue when a storm rolled in and rain began to pour down. After a brief shutdown, the stage was soaking wet, so rather than wait for stagehands, my dad and Pee Wee grabbed mops and started mopping up the water. Here are two guys, the stars of the show out there on the stage, cleaning up the mess! I wonder how many stars today would do that?

Dad and Pee Wee were two simple guys with great big hearts and never afraid to lend a helping hand. Story after story comes from beginning musicians whom they helped and encouraged. They also made a point to entertain soldiers and even went to hospitals to perform for wounded veterans. In my dad's last performing years, he also provided the homeless with some entertainment at a weekly church soup kitchen.

We could probably write a separate book filled with nothing but stories of their generosity and kindness, these two simple guys just trying to make a living.

After the divorce, every time we spent time with Dad he always tried to find something unique to show or teach us. He was not about extravagance, since he cherished the simple things in life. The following is a good example.

One time my brother and I were at his house and he decided to take us out to lunch. He didn't ask where we wanted to go, we just got in the car and as we rolled down the road, my brother and I grew curious. Dad was being awfully quiet, and as we were getting close to the destination, he asked, "You boys ever have a Whopper?"

We had never been to Burger King, since they were fairly new at the time. So we chorused, "No, we've never had one." This seemed to make Dad even more excited. We pulled into Burger King's parking lot, went through the drive through, and Dad ordered both of us a Whopper. Not the junior, mind you, this was the big boy!

Many of you may remember that when Burger King first opened, the Whoppers were much bigger than they are today, and the quality much better. Of course, Dad ordered some fries and a coke and parked the car. Then he pulled them out of the bag and handed each one of us our Whopper.

When I opened the wrapper, my first thought was, "Dad, what are you thinking? There's no way I can eat all of this." The thing covered half of my lap. But guess what? I ate every bite, including the fries. That was the best doggone hamburger I think I ever had. We probably looked like three pigs at feeding time!

To most kids, this might not have seemed like a big eventful time with your dad, but it's a memory I cherish. I will never forget the day Dad said, "You boys ever had a Whopper?"

The Man and His Music

I thought it might be of interest to share some things about my dad that most people never knew.

*My father was a very handy guy with tools.

*He was an excellent golfer. He taught my brother and I to play at a young age. It was one of his favorite pastimes.

*He was a certified public accountant. He was my tax man for years, but he eventually taught me how to do my own, and I will be forever grateful.

*He taught himself how to build handmade fiddles.

*He loved to tell jokes. He had more jokes than anyone I knew, but the funniest thing was, they were all clean.

*He almost became a preacher, but joined up with Pee Wee King instead, and the rest is history!

*He was a deeply religious man and wrote many Gospel tunes.

*You could give him an unfamiliar instrument he had never seen before, and he could play a tune on it within about five minutes.

*He was a guitar teacher in his later years and created an excellent guitar teaching video (Redd Stewart's Basic Guitar Study Course.)

*He never had any formal training in music.

*I honestly can say that I cannot remember one time my dad raised his voice in anger towards me, and I gave him plenty of reasons to do so!

*He loved to fish.

*He was an excellent pool player, and could execute several complicated trick shots, like you see the pros do.

*He taught himself how to play Bach and Beethoven on the piano and played it well.

*He liked a lot of the Beatles music and learned several of their songs. He could play the chords and melodies on the guitar all at the same time. This made it sound like two guitar players, but it was just him.

*He was a radio operator in the Army and spent a lot of time in tanks.

*He only had a seventh-grade education.

*He taught himself to be a chiropractor and used to take his table with him and adjust people's backs & necks behind stage.

*He taught himself photography, which became one of his main hobbies. He had his own darkroom and created portraits for family and friends for years.

*And best of all, he was a great dad.

When I look back over his life, I realize his tenacious drive and that he wasn't afraid to try anything. He achieved pretty much everything he put his hand to. The list above and the rest of the book bear testimony to this. If there's one thing Dad taught me, it's that you can do anything if you just try.

I still have not discovered exactly when this event took place, but
it had to have been in the mid to late '80s. This experience must
have been a special treat for my dad and Pee Wee.

Included in this show was Patti Page. It wasn't often through the
years that these three had the opportunity to share the stage, and
I believe this was the last time. My dad and Pee Wee were on the
Country-side of music, while Patti was on the Pop side.

They had a great band backing up the acts with the incredible
Johnny Gimble on fiddle, and one by one, each act gave a grand
performance. Pee Wee was first and did a few numbers on his
own with the band, and then, as always, he gave my dad a grand
introduction and enormous praise. Even later in life, Pee Wee said
he still believed Redd Stewart had the best voice in Country music.

My dad came out in his very appropriate flashy outfit and stepped
up to the microphone in a very humble but confident manner. The
first song he performed was "You Belong to Me," complete with
tradeoff solos with him on guitar and Johnny Gimble on fiddle.
Their solos drew a huge applause.

Every time I watch this video, I feel a bit of sadness because
his voice was beginning to slip. Years and years of singing were
beginning to take its toll, and he could no longer hit the notes he
used to. But as the professional he was, he pulled it off with class.
The audience's applause spoke volumes.

The next song up was *Tennessee Waltz*. Patti Page came onstage
and began singing. As she finished the song, she graciously introduced my dad and Pee Wee. Then as a trio, harmonizing together,
Patti, my dad and Pee Wee finished the song again to enormous

applause. Not often did an audience get to see the writers of the *Tennessee Waltz* and the artist who took it to the top sharing the stage.

After I watched the video, I realized that Dad's worn out voice was inevitable, and his time in the spotlight was ultimately going to come to an end. Up on that stage he was happy, proud, and still had the sparkle in his eyes that I always remembered. He was doing what he loved and enjoying every minute of it.

BASIC GUITAR STUDY COURSE
BY REDD STEWART

The home study for anyone who wants to learn to play the guitar, improve guitar skills, or learn music fundamentals.

STUDY GUIDE FOR VIDEO CASSETTE COURSE

SUPER HG. Insert this side into recorder ⬆ Do not touch the tape inside　[AVI]

REDD STEWART'S
**BASIC GUITAR
STUDY COURSE**
The home study for anyone who wants to learn to play the guitar, improve guitar skills, or learn music fundamentals

VIDEO CASSETTE
COURSE

AMBRIDGE

© 1986

The New Direction

In the 1980s, Dad began to work in a new direction. I think the things he did during this decade had been brewing in his mind for years, and now he could accomplish them. You have already seen that he loved to teach and help others achieve their dreams—this was a chance for him to do just that.

Now that he had the time, he began to teach students to play the guitar. He grew quite a class of students and began to perfect his teaching. This spawned a new idea. The VCR had become extremely popular and gave him just what he needed to put this idea together.

He developed a basic guitar course for beginners, creating all his own cue cards and writing the script for his teaching video. Then he created a workbook to go along with the video series. He drew all of the charts and artwork and hired a small production team to shoot the whole video in his basement studio.

The Basic Guitar Study Course by Redd Stewart is no longer available today, which is a shame because he put together such an effective plan.

He followed this video with another titled *Writing and Selling Your Music.* Here, he shares his experiences in the music industry and teaches viewers how to be successful in music, as well as the possible pitfalls. The industry has changed so much today, so this advice would be outdated, but at the time it implemented great advice.

Dad's new direction also included a lot more time for fun. Golfing became much more front and center. He did a lot of charity events and spent time with old friends on the golf course. Rather than traveling across the country to perform, he entertained at local golf courses, churches, restaurants, and aboard one of his favorites, "The Belle of Louisville."

The only remaining authentic steamboat from the great American packet boat era, The Belle is the pride of Louisville. It's a National Historic Landmark and an icon of the Louisville Waterfront.

At 105 years and counting, the Belle remains purely steam-powered and paddlewheel-propelled. The historic vessel provides tours up and down the river, including fine dining and onboard entertainment. My dad played there quite often, and eventually signed a three-year contract with a small group of musicians to entertain on a regular basis.

During the '80s he never stopped writing, and his heart began to turn to Gospel music. He wrote some great songs, most of which have never been released. He was beginning to focus on one final recording session, and I believe he had a longing to step into that studio just one more time.

Recycling the Music

Every artist, if successful, has his moment in the spotlight, and I'm sure they would all tell you not to waste the moment when you are there. That moment only lasts for so long.

The '50s were the golden years for my dad and Pee Wee. Through the '70s and '80s, they began to do what most artists do—I like to call it recycling your music. Though my dad continued to write, it was pretty much for future solo releases, at least that was the idea.

My dad and Pee Wee began to repackage their music into new projects. New titles for albums, along with fresh covers, made them look like a new release. The old fans love them, and this repackaging introduces their music to a new set of fans.

Over this time they released several albums, such as *The Best of Pee Wee King & Redd Stewart*, and *Pee Wee King Inducted into the Hall of Fame—1974*. This continued through the years.

Family Bear Records put out the CD release I love the most. If you ever want to hear this duo's music, this release is the one to buy. It boasts a 6-CD box set complete with an incredible book of wonderful pictures, along with a story of their entire musical career. It is top notch and a great tribute to their music. You can find this online: *Pee Wee King & His Golden West Cowboys (6-CD Deluxe Box Set)*.

Though their time in the studio and their television shows had ended, the pair continued to periodically perform at handpicked venues such as fairs and charities. Touring 252 days a year was over. Time to slow down and enjoy the fruits of their labor, plus have a shot at a halfway normal life they had never experienced before.

They could both look back over all those years and be extremely proud of what they had achieved. They wouldn't tell you this, but I say they made history!

During the '80s, as always, my dad continued to write music. As a matter of fact, he wrote until the last time he stepped into his basement studio, evident by the half-written song that still remained on his desk. Music was such a part of who he was that he just could not stop. He lived, ate and breathed music 24-7. I fully believe this is what God created him to do.

At the beginning of the '90s, he walked into South Plains College in Levelland, TX to record his very last session. He had written quite a few Gospel songs in his later years, and welcomed this opportunity to do his first Gospel album. With quite a few other songs written, he chose what he felt were the best and recorded a second album along with this Gospel album.

He titled the album *Faith in Hand*, and called the second album *Reflections of You* after its title cut. The songs he chose were well-written and produced, but the sad part was the style of music on *Reflections of You* did not fit the music of the day. *Faith in Hand*, on the other hand, was Gospel, which is timeless. However this album still had an older sound that just wasn't up to the standards of the '90s.

Fortunately, my dad's intentions were more along the line of selling these at shows. He produced them under his own record label, so I don't think he intended to release them nationwide. Both albums were released on cassettes only, because vinyl records were slowly dying.

These two albums are bittersweet to my family because by this time Dad's voice was extremely worn. Though the songs are great, it's sad to hear a voice that once was smooth as honey struggle to hit the notes. When I heard these albums, my first thought was not to share them with the public.

I didn't want people who knew him well to hear him in that condition. I didn't want this to be a representation of my dad's talent to new fans who had never heard him. But soon I realized this was a part of his story. All good things must come to an end, and that time was fast approaching.

Fortunately for me, he had recorded demos of some of these songs years before when his voice was still good. Don Powell, who just happened to be the man to set up those recording sessions, contacted me years ago and sent me copies.

Though I don't have all of the songs on these two cassettes, I do have some of the best ones, and Dad's voice shines on these recordings. Thank God for friends like Don Powell!

Rusty Hudelson, Associate Professor of Music at South Plains College, co-produced both of these albums. He also played piano on all the cuts. The following is a message he left us in the Guest Book on my dad's website. It speaks for itself.

"In 1991, Redd came to South Plains College to record two albums. I co-produced those two albums and played piano on all the cuts. Redd donated a scholarship fund to our department, and we have a Redd Stewart Studio named after him, with a bronze plaque containing his image and his biography outside the door. What a wonderful man he was, as well as one of the greatest song-writers and musicians to ever grace this planet."

~Rusty Hudelson—Associate Professor of Music, Levelland, Texas

Redd singing "The Tennessee Waltz" for the last time
at The Tennessee Fall Homecoming Festival

The Stewart Family Band performing
at The Tennessee Fall Homecoming Festival

J ust north of Knoxville, Tennessee lies a sleepy little town called Norris. Just outside of Norris up in the hills lies the Museum of Appalachia, a living mountain village. The Museum of Appalachia seeks not only to preserve physical artifacts of an earlier time; their greater mission is to instill in the community—regionally, nationally, and internationally—a greater knowledge of and appreciation for the Appalachian heritage.

The Museum offers daily self-guided tours and is available for group and school tours, educational programs, weddings, parties, corporate events, facility rentals, and more. John Rice Irwin founded this museum in 1969. It didn't take long until he added what became known as the Fall Homecoming Festival, created to include the music that came out of the Appalachian Mountains, where Country music got its start. This was a small gathering at the beginning, but eventually grew into a five-day event.

There were five stages in different locations on the property, with the main stage being attached to the restaurant. Musicians from Bluegrass, Folk, Americana and Country music came from all over the country to perform.

My Uncle Billy, who was at one time Little Jimmy Dickens' fiddle player, in his later years formed the Stewart Family Band. This group consisted of Uncle Billy on fiddle, his son Kent on guitar and vocals, his son Mark on stand up bass and vocals, his wife Helen on accordion (who once was a part of the Carter family), and a longtime friend named Tony who played the mandolin. They became a regular fixture at this festival and played there for years until Uncle Billy passed away in 2017.

My dad would occasionally travel to the festival to perform and eventually became good friends with John Rice Irwin. It was at this event on the main stage that my dad performed *Tennessee Waltz* for the very last time. It was awesome to watch because this time the band backing him was The Stewart Family Band. What a sight to see. Thank God the cameras were rolling, so we have it on video. I wasn't there to see that performance, but I sure wish I had been.

After my dad passed away, the festival held a special event in honor of him and my Aunt Helen, who had passed away shortly before. I was invited to attend and had the opportunity to stand in the very spot where Dad sang *Tennessee Waltz* for the last time, and I sang the same song with The Stewart Family Band behind me.

My Sister's Trip to the Fall Homecoming Festival

The Fall Homecoming at the Museum of Appalachia is something everyone should experience. There was so much to see and do, it was overwhelming to stand back and take it all in. My sister Lydia wrote about her experience when she was there one year, and it will give you a good feel for this festival.

"I met Uncle Billy and the rest of the group for a continental breakfast at the hotel. They were all bright-eyed and bushy-tailed and ready to start another day full of music, friends and people that could become friends at the drop of a hat. I was excited about another chance to see my Uncle and his family and friends in action, so even though I was a bit draggy, I was ready to go.

I was determined to get to the museum grounds early this morning so I wouldn't have to park so far away from everything—surely if I got there at by 8:30 there couldn't be that many people yet! Or so I thought! I guess that's how little I knew about the fans of the Homecoming festival. Amazing! I still had to park about three or four city blocks down the second row of cars that had already found their place. The makeshift parking lots are in the pastures of the farm, and when I got out of the car I was reminded of the smells of a farm. This morning was very foggy, and the grass was moist with dew. I could feel the dampness in the air.

As I walked up the long row of cars, I couldn't help but notice the license plates that were from two or three dozen different states, and I couldn't help but wonder just how many people actually attended this event. It does seem to be an interest to a vast majority of people, but then it is history. It is the history of an entire part of the country and a people who lived and worked in an area of little money but great family tradition. The people here seem to be interested in discovering their past and to make it a part of their present-day life. The music is a part of the history of these people and continues to be a part of the very soul of the land. It doesn't matter where I am on these dozens and dozens of acres, I can feel the fullness of the music and land as they meet and embrace one another.

Life was hard then. It was a struggle to simply exist. The country was backward compared to the big cities of other states. Meaningful work was scarce, and life was primitive. I shudder to think how poorly the people of today would make it under those circumstances. No cell phones, not many phones for that matter. No cable or satellite TV, much less big screen TVs. No bagel shops, no hamburger drive thru and certainly no pizza delivery. Heavens, they didn't even know what pizza was! What on earth would our kids of today do? After all the chores, they could play "kick the can" or cowboys and Indians. They could wade in the creek, or just walk in the fields or woods.

It was an amazing time in history, a time of discovery, family, and hard work. This museum and farm has done a wonderful job to preserve the buildings, the artifacts and the music of the time. I feel as though I am intruding. I feel as though I need to be quiet and respectful. Some of my family history surely must be here as well. It is to be learned and remembered.

I have made my way to the areas where they are beginning to gather in front of the main stage. There are five stages here where you can go to watch and listen and just enjoy music of a time gone by and music that continues to live today. It is nearly 9:00 am and the crowd has already begun to gather in front of the stages. It's amazing to watch this spectacle as people perch in folding chairs that don't belong to them, and then move on to other stages. There is continuous entertainment on all five stages and each group usually plays on each stage each day. Some only play a few times but groups such as my Uncle Billy and his group play every day on every stage. And when Uncle Billy isn't playing on stage, he is walking around playing with whoever needs a fiddle player. That's the way he rests. He says he will live to be 150—because he has that much fiddling left in him! It would not surprise me if he did because he sure can make that fiddle sing. His voice is still clear, and his range is still strong. His eyes are still brilliant blue and his hair white as snow. He still has the twinkle in those eyes I remember from a child. He was always smiling and laughing."

The Museum of Appalachia in Norris, Tennessee houses three museums, a restaurant, a gift shop, five stages, and numerous old-time exhibits that represent the life of early Appalachian people. On a hill towards the back of the property is a completely rebuilt village of original cabins and buildings brought from around the area to create a little village town. I never got up there to see it, but everyone said it was a sight to see.

One of the museums is a huge building filled with all types of old tools, farm equipment and old-time machinery. The second is full of history of the Appalachian people. Furniture, clothing, an old dentist chair, books, cooking utensils, tools and much more. There was so much in that one museum, it was hard to see it all in one day. The third museum was dedicated to nothing but music.

I don't think I have ever seen so many old-time instruments under one roof. The banjo display alone was incredible, and included one of Grandpa Jones's banjos. There were many instruments donated to the museum by the families of Grand Ole Opry musicians.

When I walked through all the museums and visited the numerous displays outside, I could not help thinking, "This must be my roots." I could feel the history as though I were part of it in some way. It made me wonder where my grandfather learned to make those instruments, and who taught my grandmother to play. I could not help thinking my family was connected to these mountains and the people who lived here. It gave me the feeling that I was walking on sacred ground.

Behind the main stage is a huge room where all the musicians gathered to prepare to go on stage. It was large room complete with a massive stone fireplace where a fire burned continually. We're not talking about a fireplace like one you would have in your house, this thing had to have been at least fourteen feet wide at the hearth and reached all the way to the roof on the second floor. It was the main source of heat to keep all the musicians warm.

At any given time, at least 50 or more musicians filled this room, all broken off into separate groups. Some were tuning up, some jamming, some catching up with old friends—what I called organized chaos on steroids.

One of the most amazing things about this backstage room was the collection of pictures that filled just about every space on every wall. As I browsed through them, I could not believe how many big stars had visited here—Oprah Winfrey, Grandpa Jones, Roy Acuff, Hank Williams, Jr., Ricky Skaggs, Del McCoury, and more. It made me realize how many people my dad had performed with.

Sitting back and taking it all in made me realize this was my dad's life. This was every day and every night when he was on the road performing. Not a normal lifestyle for sure. I could not help but think there was such a sad element to what I was seeing, because I knew when the show was over all these musicians returned to their lonely hotel rooms.

Each morning they would get up, pack their instruments in trucks and head to the next town. I got a bird's eye view of what my dad was going through while he was on the road, while our family was at home waiting for him to return. This is when I realized what he meant many years ago when he made me promise to never do music for a living.

In 1994 John Rice Irwin paid tribute to Dad by creating a permanent exhibit in the music museum that tells the story of the *Tennessee Waltz* and how it came to be. The exhibit has grown through the years, and now displays one of his stage outfits and shoes, his first handmade fiddle, numerous pictures representing his life, and many other artifacts. It is a beautiful display and a wonderful tribute to a man who so deserved it.

The Final Years

Redd Takes a Fall

In the mid-'90s, a seemingly not so serious fall took place at my dad's home in Louisville. He and Darlene were leaving the church they had just performed at when he slipped and hit his knee on the sidewalk. He got up, shook it off, and they continued home.

When they got to the house, he decided to take the small karaoke machine they had used at the church down to his studio. As he started down the steps, that sore knee gave out, and he tumbled to the concrete floor at the bottom. He got up and told Darlene he was fine, even though she insisted he go see the doctor.

For a little while it seemed as though this had no affect on him, but gradually, signs began to show that something was wrong. Darlene started noticing that he was dragging one of his legs and having a hard time walking. This was the beginning of a downward spiral.

As time went on, multiple complications arose that included several trips to the hospital, a hernia operation, a battle with staph infections that almost took his life, and probably more things I don't know about. Eventually he became restricted to his home, and this ended his days of performing. No longer able to go down to his studio, his writing came to an end, too.

Eventually Dad became bedridden and could no longer communicate vocally. He could communicate only by squeezing your hand once for yes and twice for no. He had become completely incapacitated.

It breaks my heart to think my dad, who had given so much to so many, would end up this way. I often think of that basement studio and all those instruments just waiting for their owner to return.

An Unwelcome Phone Call

I think just about everybody will eventually receive a phone call like the one I received in 2003. No matter how prepared you think you are, you never really are. I can remember that morning as clear as a bell. I picked up the phone to hear my sister's voice on the other end and could immediately tell something was wrong. She proceeded to tell me that my dad had passed away. My immediate reaction was probably like most people—disbelief.

Once you accept that the information you are hearing is for real, the shock sets in. After I had come to grips with the fact that my dad was no longer here, my sister continued to tell me that Darlene had passed away one week prior to Dad's death.

My family and I had moved to Virginia Beach many years before. Apparently, Darlene did not want us to know she had been diagnosed with breast cancer months before. When she finally got too sick to take care of my bedridden dad, she called her sister Joyce to step in. I will forever be in debt to Joyce and her husband Jerry for caring for Dad at that time of need. They moved into dad's house and took care of both my dad and Darlene until their last days.

It is bad enough to receive news that one of your loved ones has passed away, but two at the same time was a little overwhelming. I would like to also say how grateful I am to Darlene for taking such good care of Dad.

When she passed away, I fully believe my dad knew in his spirit that she was no longer there. I think at that point he knew it was time to go home. Though I miss him more than I can say, he is now together with his family and friends, and I am sure he is up there somewhere leading the band!

His Music Lives On

The Court of Three Stars

The Bicentennial Mall

After Dad passed away, Sharon and I began a quest to keep his legacy alive. We built the tribute website and began to reach out to people in search of anything we could find such as pictures, stories, memorabilia and videos. It didn't take long before we came up with the idea of doing a documentary about Dad's life. This was an enormous undertaking, but we felt up for the task.

We made a list of places we wanted to go and people to interview. Our first stop was Ashland City, Tennessee. I still have many second and third cousins there, so we hoped to learn more about Dad's childhood.

While we were in Tennessee, we decided to head to Nashville to shoot some video of the Ryman, Tootsie's Orchid Lounge, the Country Music Hall of Fame and Music Row. Downtown near the capitol, we stumbled across the Bicentennial Mall. What a find! We parked and started looking around, and right in the middle we discovered a place called, The Court of 3 Stars.

Picture a half circle with close to fifty bell towers boasting a combined ninety-five bells. Each tower looked to be about 20 to 30 feet tall. In the middle of the circle lay a beautiful design in marble surrounding three stars. Around the outer edge close to the towers was a raised area somewhat like a sidewalk extending almost completely around the circle. This was divided into marble tiles, each with the engraved name of a Country music star. While we were standing there in awe, the bell towers began to play, and lo and behold, we heard the *Tennessee Waltz*! We stayed and shot video of The Court of 3 Stars and realized that every 15 minutes the bells played one verse of the song, and every hour they played the entire song.

You could only imagine how I felt in the middle of that circle while I listened to those bells playing Dad's song. The Court of 3 Stars was built in 1996, so unfortunately, I don't think my dad ever had a chance to see it.

Looking back, I wish I could have taken him there. How wonderful it would have been to show him this meaningful tribute to his music. I think I would have stood next to him with my arm around his shoulder and said, "Not bad for a little old country boy from Ashland City, Tennessee."

Every time a friend or loved one passed away, we began to notice things that reminded us of them. These things were probably always there, but we just didn't notice. This is exactly what happened after my dad passed away, only to a larger degree. Not only was it happening to me, but to Sharon as well. It seemed like every time we turned around, one of us was coming home with a story. Let me explain.

First of all, one of us kept hearing *Tennessee Waltz* played in the strangest of places—in a bank, in the lobby of KFC, in a store. We heard it on the elevator, and best of all in Stowe, Vermont.

In 2004 Sharon's family planned a trip to Stowe, Vermont in celebration of her mom's birthday. Her mom had always wanted to visit Vermont, so the family wanted to make sure she got her wish. We picked a little ski resort town in the middle of nowhere. Stowe is a town that time forgot, like a little village in a fairytale. It was full of little shops, restaurants and museums where you fully expected to see elves working the counters.

One morning we all stumbled into a little gift shop and began looking around, when all of a sudden Sharon's mom said, "Stop, listen!" Off towards the back of the store we heard someone playing the piano. Sharon's mom asked, "Isn't that the *Tennessee Waltz*?" We walked towards the piano and came across a little old man sitting on the piano bench. Sure enough, he was playing that old familiar tune.

What were the chances of him and my family being in the same place at the same time in this little town in the middle of nowhere? I reached over and tapped him on the shoulder. He stopped playing and turned to look at me. I asked him if he knew who wrote the song, and he told me no. I told him it was my dad. He didn't respond but had a huge smile on his face.

He then proceeded to play the song without another word. I left the store puzzled, but finally came to the conclusion that he must have been Dad.

When we established the tribute website, people literally came out of the woodwork and began sending stories, memorabilia, video, pictures and more. It was incredible to see how many fans were still out there and how much Dad's music meant to them.

People reached out to us from all over the world, not just here in America. Family members from Ashland City contacted us. One was Ann Mitchell, who began to communicate with us on a regular basis.

Ashland City was building a bypass highway around the downtown area, and looking for a name for the highway. Ann approached us with the idea of presenting something that would represent my dad. She suggested The *Tennessee Waltz* Parkway, and we wholeheartedly agreed.

She presented the name to the board, which took a unanimous vote. With the highway nearly completed, Ann contacted us about the scheduled ribbon cutting ceremony, where they wanted us to represent my dad.

I will never forget Saturday, June 18, 2005, the day before Father's Day. I was highly surprised at how many people attended, a far bigger crowd than I expected, and dignitaries included the mayor, a state senator, city officials, and many family members.

During the ceremony, Ashland City Mayor Gary Norwood awarded me a beautiful, cherished plaque designating the name of the *Tennessee Waltz* Parkway. Then I had the honor of cutting the ribbon. It was an extremely proud moment for me, and I kept thinking, "What a great Father's Day gift for Dad!"

To top off the ceremony, they played the *Tennessee Waltz* while everyone danced on the new highway. What a sight, watching everyone dancing to Dad's song!

After the official ceremony, our hosts ushered us to a big picnic at the main city park. We felt like royalty, and I don't think I've ever seen so much food at one place, plus so many friendly people.

One of the best parts about this entire event was an enormous jam session that followed at the community hall. Talk about some talented people! I got to sit in with second cousins and third cousins I was meeting for the first time. Everybody played an instrument, including the smaller kids putting some of the adults to shame. Looking around that room, I began to realize just how deep my musical roots went.

We will forever be grateful for Ashland City's kindness, generosity and rolling out the red carpet to so many of our family members.

Experience of a Lifetime

I Am Blessed!

When I think about other family members and friends, I realize how blessed I really am. Most people who lose a parent are left with memories, pictures and some prized possessions. Except for home videos or maybe a tape recording, they will never get to hear their parent's voice again. My wife has only pictures and her cherished memories, since the family videos are very old and can no longer be played. Fortunately, a few were salvageable, but that is all she has.

For me it's completely different. How many people can pull up YouTube, search for their parent's name and find numerous videos? I can watch my dad perform, sing, talk and be interviewed for hours. I can hear his comforting voice, see the sparkle in his eye and that familiar smile any time I want. It's as though he's in the room with me.

Because of who he was, I now have the privilege of sharing him with the world through our tribute website, this book, his music, and my cherished memories. There are so many places I can go to reflect about Dad. We donated much of his memorabilia, his Epiphone guitar and Nudie suits, his gold record and other awards to the Country Music Hall of Fame.

What a blessing to know I can go there and see him in the history of Country music throughout the museum. His music left a mark all over the world. There seems to be nowhere his music hasn't touched.

In 2015, a cigar company named Crowned Head in Nashville, Tennessee created the *Tennessee Waltz* cigar. Here, the owner explains why.

"It was the song that was playing in the dance hall when my maternal grandfather met my grandmother. I vividly recall him whistling that tune throughout my childhood. It is a song that was made popular in 1950 by Patti Page, and has been recorded by everyone from Sam Cooke to Otis Redding to Norah Jones.

"The state of Tennessee is also near and dear to my heart. I met my wife here, my family is here, and of course, Crowned Heads is headquartered here in Nashville. Crowned Heads owes a great deal to the people of Tennessee for their support from the very beginning. And so, it is with a sincere spirit of gratitude that we present *Tennessee Waltz*.

"*Tennessee Waltz* is manufactured by My Father Cigars S.A. in Esteli, Nicaragua, and is the first Crowned Heads cigar to utilize a Connecticut Broadleaf wrapper. This unique medium-to-full bodied cigar is available exclusively in our great state of Tennessee. We hope you will enjoy this cigar that means so much to all of us here at Crowned Heads—and we thank you for your support which allows us to 'Carve Our Own Path.'"

~Jon Huber—Crowned Heads

We contacted Jon Huber to let him know we had heard of his new *Tennessee Waltz* cigar, and he graciously sent us a box, along with a matching ball cap which we keep tucked away in a memory box. How proud Dad would have been to sit back in a comfortable chair and smoke a *Tennessee Waltz* cigar!

Patti Page and I walking down the red carpet to represent The Tennessee Waltz

A once in a lifetime opportunity

Since my dad's death I have had the chance to meet people I never dreamed I would. I think I have learned more about my father after his passing than I ever knew when he was alive, and this has helped me deal with the loss.

The most exciting experience of all happened in Nashville in 2009. Whit Wells, a well-known creator of hybrid roses, began naming his floral creations after artists, songwriters, authors, television personalities, industry leaders, venues, organizations and icons who have made a positive impact on Nashville's entertainment community.

Barbara Mandrell and her friend Pat Bullard were both gardeners and came up with the idea of The Nashville Music Garden. They decided that, like the Country Music Hall of Fame, they would have yearly inductions of the roses and daylilies.

The first dedication was in September 2009. The Nashville Music Garden took root in the Hall of Fame Park, located at the corner of Fourth Avenue and Demonbreun, across from the Country Music Hall of Fame® and Museum. Celebrity hosts Barbara Mandrell and Lynn Anderson, along with emcee Ralph Emery, hosted an all-star ceremony befitting a garden created to recognize Music City's best. Mayor Karl Dean was also on hand to cut the ribbon and officially open the garden.

The marketing firm known as Kaleidoscope contacted me to ask if I would be interested in attending and representing my dad, since one of the roses was the *Tennessee Waltz* rose. Patti Page would be in attendance to represent the song as well. This was an opportunity of a lifetime, and my first chance to meet Patti in person, along with the many other stars in attendance.

When we arrived in Nashville and checked in, I was given an unexpected pass, and was quickly whisked off to the green room. I had no idea what to expect, and was met with tables set up with hors d'oeuvres and an open bar.

As I began to look around, I noticed the room was full with stars. Some of the stars were: Little Jimmy Dickens, Barbara Mandrell, Lynn Anderson, Brenda Lee, Charlie Dick (Patsy Cline's husband), Jeff Cook (Country band, Alabama), Randy Thomas (co-writer of "Butterfly Kisses"), Jett Williams (Hank William's daughter), DeFord Bailey's family, Barbara Orbison (Roy Orbison's wife), Janie Hendrix (Jimmi Hendrix's sister), Steve Kilgore (Merle Kilgore's son), Patti Page and many more.

Talk about a guy who felt like a fish out of water! I thought to myself, "What the heck are you doing here?" Just about the time I started to feel uncomfortable, Little Jimmy Dickens walked up. I had never met him, but he was a great friend of my dad. I introduced myself and the very first thing he said to me was, "How's Billy?" My Uncle Billy had been his fiddle player years ago on the Grand Ole Opry, and he still remembered him after all those years.

Gradually I began to feel better and got a chance to chat with several stars. I had taken a seat next to Jeff Cook in a small circle of people when suddenly Patti Page and her assistant came over. I introduced myself and thanked her for recording *Tennessee Waltz*. She was a wonderful lady and I will never forget having the opportunity to meet her.

With the program about to start, they came in to escort us down to the roped-off area. On the way, I was walking next to Randy Thomas and struck up a conversation. I told him who I was, and we hit it off right from the beginning. I really didn't know exactly who he was until they called him up to represent the "Butterfly Kisses" rose, and that's when I discovered he co-wrote the song. It was nice to have somebody to hang with who seemed to feel equally out of place.

Then they called out the *Tennessee Waltz* rose. Patti Page stood up and I got to escort her to the front stage to accept the honor. What a memorable moment that was, one I will never forget.

Afterwards, an incredible lunch was scheduled for us at the Hilton Hotel. Barbara Mandrell gave a wonderful speech at the beginning and started off with a beautiful prayer.

When I returned home, I researched Randy Thomas and got a huge surprise. When I was younger and had become a Christian, one of the very first Christian rock bands I discovered was The Sweet Comfort Band. Randy was their guitar player. I just could not believe that I was sitting right next to him and didn't even know who he was. We took so many pictures and video that day, so it's great to look at them and remember when I got to be somewhat of a star!

Dennis   Gene and Al

Colonel and I

Original Stewart Family Band

Slim   Larry Stewart

Music in the Blood

Writing this book has allowed me to step back and see my life from its family roots all the way until now. One common thread runs throughout everything: music is in the blood. If you had to use one word to define my family, it would be music.

Beyond my grandparents, I don't know how far back this goes, but someone must have taught them, so I'm sure the love of music goes back much further, and has been passed from one generation to the next all the way to me. It seems like everybody on my dad's side played some type of instrument, and most of them played professionally at some point.

My cousin Larry is a professional musician at Country Tonite Theater, formerly Dollywood, and Gaylord Entertainment in Nashville. A master musician, he plays twelve different instruments. Most of my family plays multiple instruments, it's a part of our DNA. Redd's nephews Mark and Kent have performed for many years in The Stewart Family Band. They have performed at the Museum of Appalachia's Fall Homecoming for more than 30 years.

Memories of My Dad

Stories of Redd

Over the years, hundreds of people have contacted us with such wonderful stories about Dad and what his music meant to them. Many are truly inspiring and I would like to share some with you now.

"I'm originally from Louisville, Kentucky and had the pleasure of being a guest in Redd and Darlene's home in 1987 while still in college. Redd was giving a friend of mine named Ted Jessup guitar lessons. They were very gracious and the nicest folks to meet. It was a pleasure. Redd played us a song he had recorded years before called The Chew Tobacco Rag. It was hilarious!"

~Eric/Nashville, Tennessee

"I had the pleasure of playing music with Redd with the Ordie Day band in Louisville, Kentucky. in the '80s and '90s. Redd was always a gas to be around, and he taught me a lot about being humble and showing respect to the people that we played for. He was a wonderful role model."

~Tom Jolly/Louisville, Kentucky

"I'm Charley Groth, a lifelong professional musician who has sung and played Redd Stewart compositions countless times over the years. I don't happen to have any of his songs on my own CDs, but I've played them on sessions for other people countless times, too. Now I feel guilty not to have recorded one! Tell you what, next CD, which I will be making with a great Country band in, of all

168

places, Prague, Czech Republic in July, I will include at least one Redd Stewart song!

"I do have a story to share with you. One night many years ago around Christmas time, I was driving through the town of Findlay, Ohio, looking for an address. It was a dark and stormy night, and I was unable to find the address I sought. Finally, I stopped in front of a small hotel on the main street of the town and went into the lobby to ask for directions.

"From the lobby I could hear faint music coming from the lounge. It sounded like an accordion was playing. You know the rest. I went in, sat down, and didn't get up again until the place closed!What they were doing there in that little town I don't remember. It seems to me now maybe they knew the hotel owner.

"I'll never forget discovering Redd Stewart and Pee Wee King in that little Ohio town in the middle of a long ago winter. Now I have told the story hundreds of times over the years, but I never thought I would tell it to members of Redd Stewart's family! Glad you have a website up for Redd. Keep up the good work!"

~Charley Groth

"One of my best memories are the shows I got to work with Pee Wee King and Redd back in the '70s. As you probably know, both were great friends of my mother and father. It was always a joy to be around them when they came to Nashville. It is people like them that made Country Music what it is today. I am honored to say that I worked with the great Redd Stewart & Pee Wee King."

~Rex Allen, Jr.—Country Music Singer

"I played steel guitar with Redd for over eight years in Pee Wee King's band, starting in 1946 at the Grand Ole Opry and continuing through 1954 on WAVE-TV in Louisville, KY. I left the business as a profession for 42 years and recently retired, resuming music as a hobby.

169

"To me, Redd was the glue that held the Golden West Cowboys together into a tight musical unit. Redd was a great musician and songwriter, and above all, was a friend and gentleman."

~Roy Ayres—former steel guitar player of Pee Wee King's Golden West Cowboys

"There are few that become so well-known and appreciated by so many. Music is a direct path to our hearts and to our soul. Redd's music has inspired those who love Country Music throughout his life, and this musical legacy will continue to be an inspiration to many more for years to come.

"Who that loves our music, has not heard the *Tennessee Waltz* and felt a twinge in their eye and felt thoughts of great love, great loss and memories of times past. Redd was a great musician who understood our hearts before knowing him."

~Gary Smith

"Redd and Pee Wee were very generous of their time to befriend a young musician from Berry Field in late 1943 & 1944, and let me warm up with them in the rehearsal room on the stage of The Ryman Auditorium under the stairs.

"I was in Nashville only a few months, but I learned a lot from the pros, and it put me in a position to entertain all over the world. I can't say enough thanks!"

~Bob Bryan (The Old Cowboy), Ft. Worth, Texas

"Started picking at 13, had a radio show by 16 and remember telling my picking partner, 'There's no better Country singer than Redd Stewart.' You know, I've listened for several more decades, and still feel the same way!"

~Dalton Roberts (Entertainer), Chattanooga, Tennessee

"I am so glad to see a website honoring this great legend and kind man. I had the pleasure of performing with Redd and Pee Wee at the WWVA Jamboree live broadcast in 1970. During rehearsal, Redd turned to the musicians, and said a line that has stayed with me all these years. He, in a very calm voice turned to the musicians and said, 'just increase the dynamics ever so slightly here,' and we immediately all got this point. Quick and to the point ... as Redd always seemed to be. I'm still in contact with one of the musicians of that time, and we still laugh and use his line!"

~Jerry Brightman (Steel Guitarist), Scottsdale, Arizona

"His songs were during his lifetime popular, but his character and love for the music has left a blazing trail of evidence that he is truthfully one of the greatest of all times. To not have Redd Stewart in the Country Music Hall of Fame would be a slammer on all of those who love and enjoy Country music. He should be listed at the top of the chart in reputation for his contribution in writing beautiful songs."

~Jack Ellenburg, Williamston, South Carolina

"I grew up listening to the golden voice of Redd Stewart. When my brothers and I made it to the Grand Ole Opry in the late '50s, I was thrilled one night to meet Redd in one of the small dressing rooms at the old Ryman.

"He was playing his guitar, and I was completely blown away by his expertise as a musician. I had only been aware of his singing ability, but he was an accomplished guitarist as well. One of the true greats of our time."

~Jim Glaser (Grand Ole Opry Member), Tennessee

"I knew Redd personally while I was with Curly Fox and Texas Ruby at the Opry in 1947. I also roomed with his youngest brother, Billy, and I would like to say that this was truly a family of great musicians, and Redd was a genuine songwriter. He was also a great showman and fiddle player. When I was quite young, if Pee Wee and his band came to Montgomery, I was there at their shows!"

~Jimmy Porter (Steel Guitarist), Montgomery, Alabama

"Redd was as fine a man as musician. I had the privilege of meeting and getting to know him back in the late '40s to the mid-'50s. I can honestly say that I never heard anyone say anything bad against him. He has touched the hearts of so many in his long career."

~William P. Noel, Lyndon, Kentucky)

"Redd was a great singer that will not be replaced in any field of music. He had a smooth, sweet voice and for certain a great writer. He was the backbone of Pee Wee King's show. I am quite sure Pee Wee knew this. He certainly will not be forgotten. I don't believe his greatness was fully captured and exposed by the Nashville music industry."

~Glenn Canyon, Bright, Indiana

"One of the first things I can remember as a kid is hearing music on the radio. As a small child I heard Redd Stewart with Pee Wee King and the Golden West Cowboys. My family always listened to the Grand Ole Opry, and later in life I heard Redd sing with the Pee Wee King Band on recordings. He was indeed a gifted songwriter.

"What a lucky man Redd was to have made his living full-time in music all his life with no day job, and of course, it must have been wonderful to have achieved fame. But to someone who has a great passion for music, just earning your living all your life in music is wonderful, fame is secondary to the person who really loves music.

"I think it was Shakespeare who said, 'All the world is a stage and we must all play our parts.' Redd had a wonderful part, a wonderful role, to play in life. He was truly a talented man who brought much music joy to millions of people."

~Robert Lee Johnson (The Guitar Man)

"I've been a fan of Redd's singing, playing and songwriting since I was young. I play Country music in a traditional style, and wish the modern songwriters featured on today's radio had 1/100 the class of someone like Redd Stewart. The difference between the

Country music of the '50s and today is like the difference between a good steak and a McNothing burger from the drive thru."

~Jay Peterson, Sedgwick, Maine

"I often reflect on the many great pioneers I've been lucky to know through the years who are gone now. It means more to me with every passing year. Many of us in the business still remember that your dad was one of the great unsung heroes who got a lot of well-deserved admiration, but perhaps not as much as he truly deserved as a singer, musician and songwriter."

~Ranger Doug (Riders in the Sky), Tennessee

"I was fortunate enough to work with Redd in 1990 for a few months in Kentucky. He was a special guest musician in a production of Big River. I couldn't believe how very kind and supportive he was of my interest in Country music, as well as learning the guitar, which by the way he gave me a copy of his instruction book and video that was very helpful, and he even went as far as sending a song that I wrote to some very prominent folks in the recording biz. I could listen to his stories of Patsy Cline and all the rest for days. He is a true legend not only for his music and songwriting, but also and just as importantly, as a kind and goodhearted man."

~Stuart May

"Gary (my husband) was performing one night and after he sang *Tennessee Waltz*, an audience member piped up to say that when he was in the service (he was from Tennessee), his unit was stationed in Baltimore, Maryland, and whenever they heard *Tennessee Waltz* come on the radio or the jukebox, his entire unit would stand up and salute!"

~Reva Nichols, Nashville, Tennessee

"I will always be a fan! I had planned a show with Pee Wee King years ago, and he got under the weather and it never came together. I met him (by phone) through a mutual friend of ours, George Hanes, who since then has passed away.

"I am proud of the Country music industry most of the time, but at other times I'm ashamed of how easily we have forgotten the people who paved the road ahead and who worked so long and hard to give Country music its place in American history."

~Homer Joy, Oklahoma

"My acquaintance and friendship with Redd and Pee Wee began in the late '50s, when I was a regular on the Ozark Jubilee. We became friends and worked many, many shows together, and in the later years even booked them on some shows.

"They were wonderful, talented people, and I've always said Redd was one of the most underrated people in the music business. The general public had no idea how good he was! It was a privilege to have known him."

~Leroy Van Dyke—Country Music Entertainer

"I played piano on a couple of shows with your dad in 1985. I was in Marty Martel's band at that time. We were in Lancaster, Ohio. I treasure the memory of getting to perform on stage with Redd and Pee Wee. Such great professionals, and a couple of the finest gents I have ever met in the music business. I still have a tape of that show and play it often. So much talent bundled up in one person. Write, play, sing, comic!"

~Jimmy Williams, Tennessee

"As a friend of Redd's sons Colonel & Billy in the late '60s, I had the opportunity to meet Redd several times. He was always a gracious and humble man, considering his incredible achievements in music.

"Although his songwriting is most often mentioned, he had a golden voice and excellent phrasing. His work is truly timeless. Far too little of his work is currently available. I look forward to the release of the CDs that are in the works."

~Bill Riddle

Music has been a huge part of my life and has been a special friend when I needed it. I consider myself blessed to be a part of such a talented family, and to have been given the gift of music.

Though my dad won many awards in his lifetime, there is one honor he never received. The music industry for some reason seemed to think of him as Pee Wee King's sideman, but that was far from the truth. Dad and Pee Wee King were a partnership formed many years ago. I think it is evident by the information here that one without the other did not work.

My dad contributed a lot to the Country music genre over the years, was an established solo artist, had his own television show, and in my opinion was one of the pioneers of Country music. In the Country Music Hall of Fame, you will find a plaque for Pee Wee King and J.L. Frank.

If this were a fair world, my dad's plaque would be hanging between the two. I have often asked myself why the man who penned *Tennessee Waltz*, Tennessee's state song, has not been inducted into this Hall of Fame. As you see below, I am not the only one that feels this way.

"I think the Country music songwriters of the '50s, like Redd Stewart, lit a fuse that helped Country music explode in the following decades. Those songs were fabulous and were a powerful influence in the development of Country music.

"*Tennessee Waltz* became a mega-hit when Patti Page recorded it. You could not turn on the radio or go to the dance on Saturday night without hearing this song. It's impossible to measure the long-term positive effect of Redd's songs on Country music, but it was major and Redd belongs in the CMHOF."

~Jim Flynn, Lewiston, Maine

"A Country Music Hall of Fame without the prince of Country Music, Redd Stewart, is like washing your feet with your socks on. It just doesn't work. Redd Stewart's induction into the CMHOF is long overdue."

~Nancy, Alabama

"What do you think Ernest Tubb's reaction would be if he knew that the writer of the timeless *Tennessee Waltz* was excluded from the CMHOF? I imagine he would be shocked and saddened to make such a discovery.

"If we don't recognize and honor men of stature like Redd Stewart, who helped mold and shape the world of Country music, then how will generations to come ever understand or appreciate the history and roots of the music? Redd Stewart should be honored for his lasting contributions to the honest, full bodied flavor of pure Country music."

~Janice Holland, Cape Girardeau, Missouri

"Redd, a pioneer trailblazer and legend in his own time. Setting the stage for so much music to follow. It is impossible to gauge the impact of one man on all music, but Redd's definitive sound and musical styling has set him high on the influential list with the likes of Presley and the Beatles.

"Defining songs and artists of any generation are just that, generational and don't come along often. An inclusion in The Country Music Hall of Fame is not only an honor, but in the case of Redd, a necessity to ensure the icons and true talent in music are shown off to the world they changed."

~Keith Thompson, Guelph, Ontario, Canada

"Writing the *Tennessee Waltz* alone should get Redd into the Hall, not counting all the many other things he did for the industry."

~Little Jimmy Dickens

"Redd Stewart should be in the Hall of Fame for the many years he

entertained people. He was given the gift to write the song, *Tennessee Waltz* and many other songs he helped to put on the airwaves. A great tradition of our Country music and he well deserves the honor."
~Cecil Edmunds, Waterford, Michigan

"Redd Stewart belongs in the Country Music Hall of Fame. He was the wind beneath Pee Wee King's wings."
~Shirley A. Dawson, Madison, Wisconsin

"His character and love for the music no money could buy. He had a natural knack and feeling that only comes from within, when it comes to songwriting and being a musician. He should be in the Country Music Hall of Fame."
~Jack D. Ellenburg, Willamston, North Carolina

"The compliment of stars in the Country Music Hall of Fame cannot be complete until you have inducted the co-writer of the state song of Tennessee, the *Tennessee Waltz*—Redd Stewart."
~John Bodin, Southern Productions, Wray, Georgia

"How can you not put this extra ordinary talent in the Hall of Fame? His talents and songwriting ability are irreplaceable. His many accomplishments warrant his admission. Songs like *Tennessee Waltz* will live forever. He should be honored for this with your admission to the Hall of Fame!"
~Sharon Collier, Missouri

"Redd Stewart is an icon in Country music. He has all the prerequisites for induction into the Country Music Hall of Fame. Let's make it happen!"
~Mary Mulholland, Ft. Worth, Texas

"A person who has made the contributions he has deserves inclusion in the Hall of Fame."
~Col. Walt Johnson

THE REDD STEWART STORY

"As the writer of such great standards as *Tennessee Waltz* and "Bonaparte's Retreat" and his lifetime of contribution to Country music, Redd Stewart should have been in the Hall of Fame long, long ago."

~Robert Russell, Ashely, Ohio

"If there is no other song written by him, then *Tennessee Waltz* would be sufficient reason to honor him. That is, however, obviously not the case at hand. Redd's many contributions in voice and word of song to the Country music industry have had and will continue to have a tremendous impact on the industry.

"Without doubt, he is most deserving of his rightful place of recognition in the Country Music Hall of Fame. I look forward to seeing this become a reality in the near future."

~BJ Kelly, Billings, Montana

"Redd Stewart was a true Country original entertainer and never forgot his roots that should have been in the Country Music Hall of Fame long ago. What a great singer and songwriter that has been overlooked too long and it's time he be inducted into the Country Music Hall of Fame."

~Clarence Moss, Edmond, Oklahoma

"Redd was multi-talented and deserves to be there, plain and simple. It should not even be a question. He was a pioneer and will long live in the hearts of Country music fans."

~Norman Wade, Tennessee

With the lifetime and significant contributions that Redd Stewart has made to Country music over the years, if he doesn't deserve a place in the Country Music Hall of Fame, no one does. Give him the honor and put him in his rightful place with the other greats of Country music!"

~Lloyd Johnson, Yakima, Washington

"Redd deserves a place in the Country Music Hall of Fame. He gave his life to the music he loved, and that music will continue to provide enjoyment to countless numbers of people for generations. His melodies and lyrics represent Country music as it is meant to be played and heard. I'll always treasure the times I heard him in person."
~Bob Mitchell, Louisville, Kentucky

"In my opinion Redd Stewart was one of the best singer/songwriters ever. I used to listen to "Bonaparte's Retreat" all the time when I was a child, and I will never forget it. Redd belongs in the Country Music Hall of Fame as one of the best."
~Connie Goodson, Ohio

"Redd was truly one of the greats of Country music. I can still hear him sing my favorite, "You Belong to Me." Redd should be in the Hall of Fame. He should have been put in the same time with Pee Wee King."
~Jim Blankenship, Borger, Texas

"He should have been in there a long time ago for the many classics and roots of today's Country he has written."
~Pete, New York

"In my opinion Redd Stewart is a Country music legend and has earned the right to be included in the Hall of Fame."
~'Lefty' Frank James, Wisconsin

"I see no reason as to why Redd has not already been inducted! The Hall of Fame directors must be sleeping on the job!"
~Dale W. Adam, Sr., Lebanon Junction, Kentucky

"Redd Stewart needs to be in the Country Music Hall of Fame. The man was a legend in his time and needs to be recognized."
~Earl Edwards, Allentown, Pennsylvania

"I never had the chance to meet Redd, but I felt like I knew him. *Tennessee Waltz* has always been one of my favorite songs. Here at our record label, we record a lot of traditional Country music, but nothing competes with this song. I think that if anyone deserves to be in the Hall of Fame, it should be Redd."

~Ed Gowens, North Georgia)

"Yes, for sure! Add my vote. If I could clone myself, *she* would vote for him, too. Great talent!"

~Ruthie Steele, Nashville, Tennessee

Tennessee Waltz, a beautiful song. I can't believe the writer of the state song of Tennessee is not in the Hall of Fame."

~Lloyd S. Cornelius, Honea Path, South Carolina

"Redd has paid his dues, and I feel he should be in the Hall of Fame. He has written some great songs that have been recorded by many well-known artists. I'm just sorry I never had the pleasure of meeting Redd in all my years on the road with George Jones & Tammy Wynette."

~Sonny Curtis, Columbus, Ohio

"It seems to me that Pee Wee King gets a lot of recognition for work that Redd did. I guess because the band was Pee Wee's, it overshadowed Redd's accomplishments. He should have been put into the Hall of Fame along with Pee Wee. Let's correct this."

~Kitty Bierbaum, LaGrange, Kentucky

"I knew Redd Stewart for 54 years. I shed a tear when Frank 'Pee Wee' King was inducted into the Country Music Hall of Fame. I also shed a tear that Redd Stewart was not inducted at the same time.

"I loved Pee Wee, and never knew life without him, however, there well may not have been a Pee Wee King without a Redd Stewart. Give him his true due in the Country Music Hall of Fame."

~Chris Taylor, Ashland City, Tennessee

Family Reflects

Growing up the child of a famous musician is far from the normal family life one would expect. What others take for granted, I cherish! As I look back over the years, I see a life of sharing my father with the rest of the world. Things that other kids do every day with their fathers, were luxuries for me. Traveling for eight to nine months out of the year does not leave a person much time for his family.

But the joy and pride I feel whenever I think of Dad makes all I have missed somehow worthwhile. Though my father was unable to be at my side every step of my life, he made sure to teach me some of the most important lessons in this world by living a life that could mold me by example.

I always watched my father from a distance and learned from the things he would do and say. Like an artist painting scenery, I would study him in detail and try to recreate his personality in me because I admired him so much. He was probably one of the kindest people I have ever met.

Full of life, always had a joke, always giving, and never had an unkind word for anyone. I do not think I have ever seen him angry it just was not in him! He had an incredible faith in God, and a love and passion for music that manifested itself in the wonderful music he has left us.

As a young boy I would watch in amazement while my father played his guitar. His fingers would dance across the strings creating beautiful music that would grab the attention of all who were around him. He was truly an entertainer and would leave you feeling better about life and yourself no matter what your circumstances.

I am a better man for having known him and thank him for being my father. As I have always shared him with you through my life, I will continue to share him now and forever. May he touch your life as he has mine. I love you, Dad. Save me a seat in the band.

~Billy Rae Stewart (Redd's youngest son)

What a kind, gentle-spirited man he was. Always had a kind word about others, and never, ever raised his voice. When I think of Redd, warm memories always come to mind. The most vivid memory I have, that I personally will always treasure is when we were at Redd's house visiting, and Redd's wife, Darlene, her sister Joyce, my two daughters Allison and Jenny, Billy (Redd's son) and I were all sitting around the kitchen table talking and laughing.

After a while I noticed that Redd was missing and when I looked up, I saw him standing in the doorway, looking over at everyone around the table, with the most beautiful look on his face. He was looking straight at his son Billy with the most proud, love-filled look a father could possibly have for his son. You could just see the love and pride he had for him. I will never forget that look in his eyes.

I also have many memories of other times when visiting Redd that evolved around music. There was a time I remember when we were all in the living room. Redd was playing on his grand piano, Billy was playing guitar, Lydia (Redd's daughter) was playing the banjo, and Colonel (Redd's other son) was playing a guitar. I was so amazed at the talent that came from one family and how they could just feed off each other and carry on for hours! What a musically talented family!

Yet another time visiting, we all headed down to Redd's home studio in the basement of his house. It was around Christmas time and we all decided to get in the spirit! Redd had his fiddle out, Billy had the guitar, and Darlene, Joyce, my daughters, and I all joined in singing Christmas carols.

They recorded everyone singing and having such a fun time! Those old tapes were recently discovered when they cleared everything out of his studio. One of these days we may be able to share those with you on his tribute website.

You could always count on having a fun-filled, loving time whenever we were all together. Redd always made sure that everyone felt welcome and there was always plenty of love to go around. I feel extremely blessed to have met Redd's son, Billy. He is a carbon copy of his dad, and has that same gentle, kind, patient spirit that Redd had.

Thank you, Redd for giving me such a beautiful person to spend the rest of my life with. I love and miss you."

~Sharon Stewart (Redd's daughter-in-law)

What do you say about a man who always seems to think of others? As a kid growing up I can't really think of any bad memories, many good ones though! He was always there for us kids and made sure we had our wants and needs. He had a firm hand in his teachings, but always with a loving and kind heart.

Dad always had a way of making things simple. I remember me wanting to be that professional golfer. I always had to have the biggest and best set of clubs. Well, he bought me that set and then would take me and my brother Billy golfing. He had an adjustable club with a key he wore around his neck. He beat us both every single time! He would say, 'Son, it's drive for show and putt for dough!' I guess in a way I learned from those things he taught us.

Dad gave me the talent of playing several musical instruments, how to understand music, and sing, and I played all the taverns, nightclubs and bars years ago. He always told me, don't follow what I do, but be your own man.

Being on the road as a musician is a hard life, and need I say I took his advice. I guess because of him, I have always led a simple life. I am always thinking back as how dad would handle this? Yep, a lot of great memories about a wonderful man that I am proud to call my Dad.

Now that I am up in my years, I can understand my dad much

better now. It puts a smile on my face every time I think of him. Dad's music did that for people worldwide! He always stayed in the background, but really was the main backbone. I love you Dad. Wonder if St. Peter knows what that key is around your neck?

~Colonel Henry Redd Stewart, Jr. (Redd's oldest son)

There is a tiny pocket in a corner of my heart that has provided a safe place for treasured memories and feelings. I have known of this pocket for most of my 60 years and have always wondered if others are as blessed as I to have such a special place to frequent. It is always with me and at any moment, I am able to reach down deep inside and pull out a memory and relive that special moment. It is special place to me and one I visit often.

When I was a little girl, I was raised to believe in things I could not see—like God, and love, and the belief that my father was with me even though he was many miles away. I mastered this ability very easily as I was a trusting child and found it very comforting whenever he would be away from me for weeks at a time. Even now, as an adult, I still believe in things I cannot see. I cannot see the wind, or God, or my father, but I know they exist as I can see their impact on everything around me.

This pocket in my heart is so very tiny but holds a lifetime of memories I choose to protect and keep near. Most of these memories are of my father and so as a tribute to him, I hope people have enjoyed and learned about the life of the entertainer, the musician and songwriter, but most of all my father."

~Lydia Stewart Morrow (Redd's daughter)

Also Available From

WordCrafts Press

Geezer Stories: The Care & Feeding of Old People
by Laura Mansfield

An Introspective Journey: A Memoir of Living with Alzheimer's
by Paula Sarver

Against Every Hope: India, Mother Teresa, and a Baby Girl
by Bonnie Tinsley

Confounding the Wise: A Celebration of Life, Love, Laugher & Adoption
by Dan Kulp

Pressing Forward
by April Poytner

Fortunate Son: The Story of Baby Boy Francis
by Brooks Eason

www.wordcrafts.net

CPSIA information can be obtained
at www.ICGtesting.com
Printed in the USA
LVHW080159060121
675858LV00023B/147/J